THE
LEADING LADY

HER LIFE AND HER INFLUENCE

Marjorie O Esomowei

authorHOUSE®

AuthorHouse™ UK
1663 Liberty Drive
Bloomington, IN 47403 USA
www.authorhouse.co.uk
Phone: UK TFN: 0800 0148641 (Toll Free inside the UK)
*   UK Local: (02) 0369 56322 (+44 20 3695 6322 from outside the UK)*

Published by AuthorHouse 06/01/2022

ISBN: 978-1-6655-9823-1 (sc)
ISBN: 978-1-6655-9845-3 (hc)
ISBN: 978-1-6655-9824-8 (e)

Library of Congress Control Number: 2022908457

Print information available on the last page.

This book is printed on acid-free paper.

FOREWORD BY REVEREND CLEM ESOMOWEI

I have gone through the book 'The Leading Lady, Her Life and Influence.'and I find it very insightful and beneficiary to all ladies who aspire to lead or are already at the helm of affairs in all spheres of life. I have been married to Pastor Marjorie for 36years and we are privileged to lead together since 1995 till date. I see in the book 'The Leading Lady, Her Life and Influence a sincere presentation of her years of leadership in the various organisations she has led including a Merchant Bank subsidiary. She has highlighted the principles leading to her success in the corporate world, Church and service to God and humanity in Europe, Africa, Canada and the United States of America. She makes it clear that focus, forthrightness, determination and fair-play are very instrumental to effectiveness and efficiency as a leading lady. Pastor Marjorie has written several books including Children Are Like Olive Plants, Overcoming in Gilgal, 33 Tips for Single Ladies, A-Z of the Multipurpose Woman, No by More Curse, Designed for the Palace and Inspirational Business Ideas which have been a strong foundation for writing her new book ' The Leading Lady, her Life and Influence.' She enumerates the importance of getting a life in the midst of a busy leading life in her corporate world creating a beneficial balance for optimum productivity. I recommend 'The Leading Lady, Her Life and Influence' to everyone especially ladies who aspire to make positive impact in the corporate world and society at large.

Reverend Clem Esomowei
Pastor Author Mentor

FOREWORD BY ARCHBISHOP CHARLES AGYINASARE

Powerful book, inspiring, enlightening and motivating. It is a book that is designed to lift the head of any despondent and lugubrious lady to face LIFE.

It is designed to turn the fearful into a bold and achieving lady. The Leading Lady, Her Life and Influence would empower the ill-equipped to rise up and be counted as a leader to her generation.

Get this book now and get one for a friend, it would revolutionize your life.

His Grace Archbishop Charles Agyinasare
Pastor, Chancellor, Author and Statesman

FOREWORD BY DR. CINDY TRIMM

When you think of business, social and civic leadership, what image comes to mind? Is it a man in a suit, one with a stethoscope around his neck, or perhaps a clergyman with a turned-back collar? Growing up, I would have probably conjured up in my mind a mental picture similar to the ones hitherto described as well. But today, my mind thinks differently. Women have made incredible strides not only in the business space but in every industry arena.

Although women have made significant strides, we still are underrepresented. This trend is changing, though.

In this book, Pastor Marjorie Esomowei presents a compelling case of why a woman should arise to take their place in leadership without compromising their femininity. She takes an intelligent approach that I believe will inspire women from all walks of life and encourage them to be a catalyst for change.

While women have been and continue to play a critical role within the workforce, it's only recently that women in leadership have been embraced as a human resource preference. The data is clear that organizations with significant representation of women outperform those with a more homogenous leadership, i.e., C-Suites, board membership, etc.

Additionally, it has been proven that when women are supported in their quest to progress, families, communities, industries, and eventually nations move too (e.g., China). To fight for women is to fight for humanity, and to unleash the potential in women is to release the potential in society.

It is encouraging to observe that women are still succeeding despite gender-discriminating barriers.

Using biblical examples and recent case studies, pastor Esomowei skillfully pulls out principles that will help women redefine how to show up unapologetically powerful in businesses, ministries, industries, and government as a solution to world problems. She is a gritty, honest, and dynamic writer, and I am confident you will enjoy her fresh perspective.

Dr. Cindy Trimm
Author, Mentor, Business Leader

DEDICATION

I am dedicating this book THE LEADING LADY HER LIFE AND HER INFLUENCE to my first and foremost Mentor and Coach, the Sweet Holy Spirit. Thank you for making a worthy vessel out of me.

And to the Husband of my youth Reverend Clem Esomowei, thank you for being my most stable cheer leader. I love and appreciate you honey.

To Women across the Globe who are taking bold steps each day to fulfil their God given Destiny. I celebrate you all.

ACKNOWLEDGEMENT

No good thing happens single handledly. Fulfilling Destiny and Purpose is a mixture of all the events of our life and the people that we meet during our life journey.

My first thanks goes to God the Father, the Son and the Holy Spirit. Through you I daily run through troops and leap over walls. I am grateful to be called a child of God and a minister of the Most High God.

My husband Reverend Clem Esomowei, Honey thanks so much for always making yourself available to answer my one million questions. (Those who know me are aware that I can ask one million questions within an hour). You are my number cheer leader! I will choose you again and again.

Archbishop Charles and Mama Vivian Agyinasare thank you for being great role models for Christ and impacting my life and ministry through your verbal and non verbal exemplary Christian lifestyle. It would seem like I am forever asking one question or the other but patiently you answer all of them. Thank you sir and thank you ma.

Dr Cindy Trimm, you simply amaze me with your promptness to my requests. You aren't just a minister of the gospel to me, you are a godly inspiration to me. Thank you ma for your authentic life.

Triumphant Church International World Wide, thank you.

All the associates and partners of Wisdom For Women International, Wise Women Awards and Wise Women Pray, you have made Ministry joyful and easy for me.

Power Base Prophetic Intercessors Platform, you have become a very valuable part of my extended God family. I actually wish I could list everyone's name here. You ladies are simply the best.

Last but not the least, My mum Comfort Kemmer and my dad Chief O W Amachree, I truly wish you both lived to see this day! You gave me the best of yourselves and never failed to remind me that I am a STAR!.

And to you reading this book! A big Thank you. I love and appreciate you

CONTENTS

WHY YOU SHOULD READ THIS BOOK?

I have written this book for any woman who is in Ministry and in Leadership. You will find it beneficial no matter your level so older women who have great level of experience and new entrants will definitely find this extremely useful.

I have tried to pack so many years of experience into this space. My heart has always desired to help as many women as possible within the faith to do God's work in excellence and to enable the Church work more efficiently.

CHAPTER ONE

. . . . ❖ . . . .

WHO IS A LEADING LADY?

Most leadership books would give you varied definitions of a leader and their admirable qualities but there is no one true definition to explain that because all leaders are unique and leadership is viewed from different perspectives.

For me, one of the greatest definitions I ever heard was from the founding chairman of The Leadership Institute at the University of Southern California, Warren Bennis. He said,

"Becoming a leader is synonymous with becoming yourself. It is precisely that simple and it is also that difficult." – Warren Bennis.

What he is telling us is one of the most important definitions of who a leading lady is. She is taking a lead position within her circle of influence, while on a journey of finding her innermost self. A woman who, at the same time as leading others, is working steadily on discovering herself to become the best version of herself she can possibly be.

Refusing to be captured in another person's body, she resists all and any temptation of being any other woman, no matter the pressure she feels to do so. The leading lady is a woman steering her purpose forward through her authentic self.

There are many women who have found themselves in leadership positions where they have not quite understood that to do anything substantial or significant in life, they would first have to BECOME.

I will be discussing more about the leading lady and her BECOMING, as it is that which forms the bedrock of her LIFE and her INFLUENCE.

You will see that I have carefully avoided defining who a leading lady or leader is and this is because I will not lure you into the trap of thinking one size fits all. How could it be when we are all unique?

I believe that has been the challenge many leading ladies have faced in the past and will continue to do so today unless they realise it is a mistake to allow others to label them and determine what they should be doing and how they should lead. When a leading woman does not make the effort to understand herself and the leadership journey she is on or recognise her own style when leading others, she will fall into the trap of having a title without any influence whatsoever and what good is leadership without influence? Leadership IS influence.

A leading lady, therefore, would be someone who knows and loves herself. She understands her worth, her assignment and her life purpose and she takes the time to properly connect with all that God has assigned for her as it will not only support and lift her, but those around her also.

She is never in competition with another woman but only herself as she walks the road along her leadership journey.

You may also have noticed that I have not talked about titles or hardcore qualifications that a leading lady needs, as I believe from the depth of my heart that, ANY woman can be a leading lady.

Any woman can choose to be a positive leader to influence many or even one at a time.

This she can accomplish without any formal title or training simply by accepting her God given purpose.

This does not mean that titles are bad, it simply means they do not have to be the main stay of someone who is an example to others.

Guess what? whilst writing the above statement, I physically sighed in relief; like this is it! It makes me so glad that any woman whatsoever can be a leading lady and the thought of it makes me leap in my heart.

She just needs to understand and pursue her journey of leadership by regularly training and grooming herself to becoming her God ordained self and being fully aware that, as she leads others, she is also on a journey to becoming.

With this in mind, no leading lady should ever feel unqualified, intimidated or incapable of playing her role as a leader. She would rather understand that though being criticised, judged and defined inappropriately, that she is on a journey of getting better, being better equipped and doing better. This removes all the barriers and limitations etc. As she emerges, she knows that people's judgement change just as culture, social and individual prejudices change.

There will always be a core of people who believe that you are their leader, although they know and understand you are on a journey of becoming. It is a journey toward perfection, although nobody ever gets there as that is a lifelong pursuit.

Proverbs 4: 18 amplified

"But the path of the just (righteous) is like the light of dawn that shines brighter and brighter until [it reaches its full strength and glory in] the perfect day".

A leading lady then, would also be a woman that knows that God called her and her first accountability is to God before others.

CHAPTER TWO

. . . . ❖ . . . .

SHOULD A WOMAN LEAD?

It is a lifelong question that has plagued earlier generations and it still plagues women in all spheres of life to date. Many people don't talk about it but from their actions alone, you will know that there are many who do not believe a woman should take a lead at all, not ever. If she should, then those same people would think, it ought to be at a low level and should only involve her doing not very important things - mindless pursuits even.

This is a problem most women face, not just in the male dominated industries, but in most of life's domains. It is a major problem and so much so, that most women ask, 'HOW DO WE DEAL WITH THE ALPHA MALE?'

And if that is a problem now, then what about the women who come after us? How will the next generation deal with the alpha male? Some men who feel no women should lead.

I'm sad to say that most people you meet really don't have an answer to this because either they can't admit that the alpha male even exists or, it is so deeply ingrained in them that it is almost a taboo subject as if it were sacrilege to even talk about this.

This is a question that still plagues the Church and even most of those in Government circles.

For instance, recently, there was a Nigerian ruler who openly reprimanded his wife for making her political opinion known to the public. Not only that but his description of her was this: " My wife belongs to the kitchen, the living room and the other room" … whatever that other room means (I think we can guess).

Another example would be from a recent Crans Montana Forum in Europe, who graciously set up a forum for African women in leadership. There, a top male representative from one of the countries was invited to speak at the forum and he shocked everyone when he openly stated that women cannot be in leadership because of the risks involved. He explained it like this:

"When men keep women away from leadership, it is their way of protecting them from danger."

Can you believe that? Fortunately, as the speaker who followed him, I had the chance to give him my opinion and in public. "SIR", I said, "You err on this one". I was not the only woman to reprimand him that day as many other women there did the same and all with the good manners and politeness befitting a lady.

I am totally in disagreement with statements such as these and many like them that I have heard over the years and my personal belief is that God created us all equal in nature. What that really means to me is that God did not create any lesser being between the male and female gender. Yes, I totally agree that biblically, in purpose, hierarchy and assignment, the husband should take the lead because of order and because, that is the God ordained way but no lesser human beings have been created.

The bible is very clear about the Godly, biblical and scriptural stance on this matter and so, I wonder where the argument is coming from?

Galatians 3:28 NLT

'There is no longer Jew or Gentile,[a] slave or free, male and female. For you are all one in Christ Jesus.'

5

If a future leading lady has a proper understanding of this concept, then it will truly prepare her to lead from a wholeness perspective and, without an inferiority complex.

No woman should allow culture, religion or any individual's bias to ever downplay or limit her, as she pursues her life assignment.

I had the privilege to work with a group of church leaders in a consortium where I was the only woman. From the outset, I knew it was going to be difficult because of their attitude and on one occasion, they actually held a meeting behind my back. Of course, I was tempted to fight back but I was also conscious of the consortium goals and so, on every occasion, I held back my *fight*. Tell me, how many leading ladies have had to pull back their fight too and pull back their strength, because they do not want to be labelled 'AGGRESSIVE', which is normally the outcome of such behaviour.

How many times have we had to pull back for the fear of that or being called forward or too much like a man? Each and every time a leading lady pulls back like this, a project suffers, the church suffers and the kingdom of God loses.

We don't have to look at research papers or formal statistics to know that women form a large percentage of the church population and as I have always said, when we ignore women's involvement in the church of our Lord Jesus Christ and the training/ empowerment of women, we have downplayed the greater part of the Lord's workforce.

So, how can this message be swallowed up by the alpha males who form the majority of the church leadership population? How can it be imbibed by the other kingdom and the church women who *kill* the rising female stars and those still rising in the kingdom?

Each time you talk about a leading lady like that or fight one, you cause the kingdom of God to lose because, many times, leading ladies will draw back their hands. Nobody wants to be labelled aggressive, especially when they are simply being assertive.

Myself, as a leading lady, I have many times had qualms with men and sadly even women, who have done everything possible to drag me down.

So, the big question is, *how do we deal with the alpha male in the church and in our workplaces?* And how do you deal with other women who think just because you stride, you are proud?

The first question to ask is, does this alpha male even exist in the church? Was Paul the Apostle an alpha? Did he have a problem with women and did he feel that women must not speak in church?

And is being an alpha male a bad thing or is it necessary? Well, in my opinion, it is not a bad thing and yes, it is necessary. Is every strong Christian male leader an alpha? No! Not all male leaders in leadership are alphas.

I will endeavour to touch on each of these issues as we go through this book.

Yes, I will say that the Alpha Male exists. God blessed the church of the Lord with very strong male leaders so that they could accomplish his kingdom work here on earth.

'The glory of young men is their strength.' Proverbs 20:29"

There is no doubt that some men have crossed the border lines and ignored the exhortation of Galatians 3: 28. I say that each time you stop a woman from serving Christ in this way, you wound the body of Christ.

But back to the question, was Paul the Apostle an alpha male?

I can tell you he was a strong leader who achieved a lot for the Kingdom of God but he was definitely not against women.

'8 For man did not come from woman, but woman from man; 9 neither was man created for woman, but woman for man. 10 It is for this reason that a woman ought to have authority over her own[b] head, because of the angels.

7

[11] Nevertheless, in the Lord, woman is not independent of man, nor is man independent of woman. [12] For as woman came from man, so also man is born of woman. But everything comes from God.'

1 Corinthians 11: 8- 12 NIV

'Apostle Paul had no qualms with Priscilla or Aquila and he began to speak boldly in the synagogue. When Priscilla and Aquila heard him, they took him home with them and explained to him more correctly the Way of God.'

Acts 18: 26
Good News Translation.

Priscilla and Aquila were the ones who taught Apollos God's word correctly.

'I send greetings to Priscilla and Aquila, my fellow workers in the service of Christ Jesus.'

Romans 16:3 Good News Translation.

Apostle Paul referred to both of them as fellow helpers, not just Aquila.

'Salute Philologus, and Julia, Nereus, and his sister, and Olympas, and all the saints which are with them.

Romans' 16:15
King James Version.

Philologus and Julia appear to be a ministry couple who worked with Apostle Paul

'Salute Andronicus and Junia, my kinsmen, and my fellow-prisoners, who are of note among the apostles, who also were in Christ before me'.

Romans 16:17

As we can see, Andronicus and Junia were a couple whom Apostle Paul described as 'Apostles of note'.

Were all these female Apostles and Leaders teaching women only? The answer to that I shall leave to your discretion but I say CERTAINLY No.

The verse below has been a real bone of contention but to my understanding, it, like every other verse, must not be read out of context. The BIBLE society BIBLE course states that every scripture read out of context is a con. I like that statement.

So, let us look at this in context. What law? What about women who have no husbands. Who do they ask?

As I write this, I am giggling. Think about all the women who serve in various capacities at church. What would happen if we all kept quiet? The church of God would be a very different place then.

'34 Women[a] should remain silent in the churches. They are not allowed to speak, but must be in submission, as the law says. 35 If they want to inquire about something, they should ask their own husbands at home; for it is disgraceful for a woman to speak in the church.' 1 Corinthians 14: 34-35 NIV

What law? There were laws in Judaism and mostly, when the law is referred to, sometimes it is in reference to those particular laws in Judaism. As an original African, I can tell you that we have many good laws that help us live a peaceful life, even before the bible was introduced to our forefathers, but we all know the traditions of men will make the word of God of no effect and so, we stick to the word of God and decipher Jewish laws from the word of God also.

As a leading woman, you were born to win, born to succeed and born to stand out and without a doubt, born to lead.

A woman is a priceless 'ornament', not only to her family but to the world at large. She is of great and immense value and she needs to know this as she takes on any leadership role. That way she can deal with all the known, unknown, seen and unseen biases and obstacles that are thrown at her.

I remember a brief conversation I had with someone when I raised the above concerns and they told me this – "Well, I thought we had gone above all that, especially as we have female Prime Ministers and Presidents in various Nations of the world".

We cannot deny or say that there aren't any breakthroughs that celebrate women in leadership both in the church and the world at large. Nor can we say that we have not shifted a little bit from where we used to be as a world but that's not to say we are THERE already.

I stand to be corrected but I have always felt that UK Prime Ministers Margaret Thatcher and Theresa May had their issues and perhaps some bad policies (every government have those) but still, I feel that just like many other women at the top, they were set up to fail. In plain language, they both had a tough time working with male counterparts and sadly some of their female counterparts too. I would take the same liberty and say that Hillary Clinton never won the Presidency of the United States of America mainly because she was a woman. This segregation exits, although it may be subtle and to understand the bias, you need to have gone through it at some level.

There is an article I stumbled upon by Stefan Stern, the co- author of 'Myths of Management'. On May 25th in 2019, he shared some similar thoughts in his piece in the Guardian online, although it was in a slightly different manner.

'In most cases, even when a woman works twice as hard as her male counterparts and her productivity and output is higher, she still gets lower pay.'

It happens frequently. For instance, in 2017, there was outrage about the inequality of staff gender pay at the BBC. The female staff were shocked when they realised the disparities between their salaries and their male counterparts.

In other news, it was revealed that Gary Lineker pockets a cool £1.8m a year. Newsreader Huw Edwards is paid £550,000, while Sophie Raworth is among the lowest-paid news presenters with a salary of £150,000. Even worse was that Newsnight host Emily Maitlis wasn't even on the list because she earned less than that".

You may think I am advocating feminism but that would be wrong. I am not. I am not even sure that I know what that word Feminism truly means. What I am saying is that the majority of our world still quietly believes that women are second class citizens.

It was only in 2019 that the Evangelical Church world woke up to a rude shock with a statement from a *leading* Evangelical preacher who asked a popular female preacher to *go home*. He continued with, "there is no case that can be made biblically for a woman Preacher. Period. End of Discussion". Hmmmmmmnnnnn! I'd almost call that ungodly! Even with the attitude with which it was said. Well from my little corner Mr Man, I'd say at least there is no biblical case against women volunteering in the Lord's army. So, to stay out of the argument, I would say I am a volunteer for the army of Jesus, just like most women are volunteers for Jesus Christ. Can all the church women volunteers say 'Amen'!

You may ask why have I taken the time to write these few lines about gender inequality etc. It is because I want you as a leading lady to know and prepare yourself for the world out there. We live in a real world where sometimes, your male counterparts will challenge you directly or indirectly. You will face opposition directly or indirectly and the woman card will be pulled on you. So, what do you do? Well, your best reply must always be 'FOCUS AND SUCCESS'. Nobody argues with success so succeed anyway!

The other issue regarding women who pull down other women is one that truly deserves a full blown book, so I won't spend time here talking about the work of *crabology*. If you are wondering what that is, the dictionary describes it as, *the study of the attitude, language and actions of individuals who refuse to support others in their effort to better themselves, community etc.* My candid advice here is that, any woman who finds herself in the midst of women crabs who are acting as friends or colleagues, change your network to a more accepting and friendly group … full stop!

CHAPTER THREE

. . . . ❖ . . . .

WHAT QUALIFIES A WOMAN TO LEAD?

Firstly, every woman is one of God's beautiful creations and she has purpose and assignment. No woman is unfruitful and without destiny and every woman is beautiful. No matter how broken and bruised she becomes, she still has a destiny to fulfil. God never creates anyone without a destiny to fulfil nor anyone who cannot fulfil theirs.

All of God's creations have hidden and untapped potential placed in them for leadership and yes, I agree that leaders are born, leaders are taught and leaders are raised.

'So, God created man in His own image, in the image of God He created him, male and female he created them'. Genesis 1:27 KJV

If I am created in God's image, whaoooo! That makes me more than qualified to lead and it does you too.

Secondly, women are created as talented creatures. According to the parable of talents (Matthew 25: 14 – 30), everyone must account for the use of their gifts and talents. So, just like the male, the female too has to give account of their talents. If you are a woman, here is your call to rise and take your place. Dear Leading Lady, you are qualified and you can indeed lead. You will one day give account of your assignment.

Thirdly, we have some great examples of successful women who, through the ages, have proved themselves to be successful leaders in many different spheres of society. We glean from their lives and we learn from them as they stand as role models to the women of today and tomorrow. These women have blessed their worlds and many are still blessing ours. Lets learn from them, they are our cloud of witnesses.

Fourthly, Old Testament and New Testament women of virtue stand as a testimony to the confidence that God reposed in women and their leadership capacities. There are examples of such women like Deborah, who was a Judge and a warrior. Sheerah who built cities. Esther who turned around the destiny of a Nation. Not forgetting the Prophetesses, Evangelists and Apostles listed in the bible. The bible records great women who made impact, worthy role models for both the women of their time and the women of ours .

We are God's masterpieces and we are all qualified to lead. Glory Halleluiah!

WHY DO LEADING LADIES FAIL AND WHY DO THEY SUCCEED?

Every leading lady needs to study other leading ladies and learn from their lives. What makes them tick? How did they achieve purpose? What mistakes did they make along the way and how could those mistakes have been avoided?

It is not the intention to name people here but I am writing in general and perhaps might mention a name or two as examples.

FEAR AND LACK OF ROLE ASSESSMENT

Two things here, firstly it is important to note, that a leading lady must not fear but instead be courageous and ready to take on assignments while taking giant strides.

Fact is, the fear of failure is the main reason why most women do not take on leadership roles.

However, it is also important that a woman does not ignore her fears as much as she must not fear. When Prophet Ezekiel came before the valley of dry bones, he prophesied hastily over them without any assessment and God quickly instructed him to circle that valley several times. Now The Prophet Ezekiel proclaimed, "It's a valley full of very dry bones". Earlier he had said it was "full of dry bones" but when he assessed his fears, he knew exactly what he was dealing with. That was VERY dry Bones.

My husband, Pastor Clem, said something recently that made me think deeply. The 22000 Israelites that turned back on the journey with Gideon, have always been preached against but we can look at their positive side. They were honest. They admitted they were afraid and not ready to undertake that journey. We too must deal with our fears because they are real and everyone fears something. If they are not dealt with, it could cripple a woman on her journey to success and attainment of influence.

When a woman does not properly articulate her strengths and capabilities, she might easily jump into a role that she is not prepared for. That said, a leading lady should not fear. No fear of the future, no fear of failure and no fear of people. The only fear she should have is of Him who has power over the body, soul and spirit. In a nutshell, *a leading lady must admit her fears but also face them.*

Many leading ladies have fallen victim to not assessing their fears and capabilities and they have quickly taken positions that men had carefully avoided, due to the imminent dangers that were perceived of the role.

That leads me on to the next point of emotions, which I will touch briefly now but deal with more elaborately in a later chapter.

Fear therefore is an issue. There have been many times when I have personally not taken leaps and pursued goals that I had in mind due to fear.

Fear of failure

What if I fail?
What if I don't make it?

What if I crash?
What if this doesn't work?

All those questions and others like them won't make any sense until you jump at your opportunity. What you should be saying is,

What if it works?
What if I succeed?
What will I do when I am a success?

Fear of what other people may say

She is a strong woman
She is aggressive because she tried to leap

The strength of a woman is meant to a positive. A plus point for her, but in the past I have experienced the effects of this negativity and have had to shy away from taking some bold steps due to the fear of being labelled 'a strong woman.'

Over the years I have realised that the strong woman label is a ploy that people use to put you down but I decided that I would pursue God's agenda for my life, no matter what anyone else thought. So long as I have the approval of the three most important personalities in my life – My God, my husband and my spiritual parents, then my light is green for 'go' and I am no longer afraid.

I am reminded of Deborah. I am reminded of Esther and I am reminded of Sheerah! They were bold women who conquered their fear.

Emotional stability

A woman is a master of emotions. This can be her biggest friend but often, her biggest enemy. A leading lady must understand the logistics of her emotions and know how to work with them for her own good and the good of her circle of influence.

All humans are emotional beings but a woman is THE EMOTIONAL BEING. As a Pastor and a Pastor's wife, I have seen important and high profile women melt under the power of their emotions when they are in love with someone. At that point in time, she is no longer able to hear you or make any intelligent decisions because she is in love.

I have often said to leading ladies that sometimes, they should not think or decide with their hearts alone but must think with their head, brains and heart, especially when it comes to matters of love and destiny. You don't want everything you have laboured for to cave in under the tag of *being in love*. Things must align properly and, in any process or state of your life, as a leading lady, you must do whatever is necessary and needful. You must take charge of your heart and your emotions, so that they don't bring you down.

We will be dealing with the subject of Emotional Intelligence further, in more detail, as I mentioned earlier but for now, let's just say that our positive and negative emotions as women should really be under control. A leading lady must not let her emotions rule her. Instead, she must be the master of her own emotions.

Being emotional is not a bad thing per se. Many have suppressed their emotions and that has been a bad thing because, thereafter they have suffered much from internal injuries. It is okay to cry. It is okay to laugh. It is okay to be angry. It is okay to be emotionally attached to people and it is okay to be in love. These things can only go wrong when they are outside of acceptable and reasonable boundaries.

Emotional wholeness is needed, just as much as physical and spiritual wholeness is for a leading lady to thrive. So, we need to be physically and mentally alert and whole. We need to think positive thoughts about ourselves and remain grateful for where life has taken us, i.e., the good, the bad and the ugly. All the experiences we have in this life make us who we are and we don't have to stress about the future and all it brings. Life itself, as we see it today, is a gift that is immeasurable.

When a woman frets about what she cannot change, she is inflicting torture upon herself and pushing herself towards emotional instability. Please do not get me wrong here; we all have days when we feel like we need a taxi to take us from one point in the house to another. Even from one room to another, but we still rise after a fall. What am I saying here? I am saying it is ok to fall but please pick yourself up again quickly because, it is simply life and that happens to each and every one of us.

Life matters

I chose to describe the above as 'life matters' because life does indeed matter. Whatever influence a leading lady wishes to make in her lifetime and after she departs it, she, needs to recognise that life will always show up for her - Family, children, husbands, sickness, love and relationships. In fact, the list is endless.

Life will often throw things at us that we never truly prepared for.

When things happen to family and friends we are affected by it because we are a part of them and they are a part of us. When this happens, we can be stalled. These things don't necessarily have to be bad. They could be either good or bad but they have the ability to affect the pace of a leading lady. When there are major celebrations, we do get distracted from our goals and aspirations but this is not necessarily bad because, like I said earlier, life just happens.

When children are at a certain age and there is no carer or support, sometimes the mother must abandon her career to look after the young ones.

When a husband falls sick suddenly, the wife is almost always the first port of call as a full-time career. Or when a husband is intimidated by the wife's success, and he subtly hinders her progress, this can stall her career path and her ambition to rise and fly. I call all these factors "life interjections'.

Sickness has no respect for anyone and just like trials can go to the house of the intercessor, the usher and the church greeter, trials also come to the house of the Pastor. When a leading lady is dealing with sickness, disease and infirmity, her career is often stalled and her role of influence could be marginalised too.

Leading ladies, just like any other women, fall in love and can fall out of love too. They too can face the heartbreak of a broken relationship etc.

When all is said, as life happens, we must understand that everyone has their own share of it. They may not say it, preferring to cover it up but we all have our own share to deal with and so, in my case, this is what I do. I remind myself that many other leading ladies have been through the same difficult path at some point in their lives and life didn't crush them. They came out on the other side. I ask God for his grace to help me through my own season of contradiction (that is when your experience contradicts the very word of God that you are standing upon) and pray to the Almighty through Jesus Christ to give me the strength to bounce back to top form. I ask for the strength and grace to carry my cross.

Unhealthy competition

I specifically took time to speak to a good number of women to ask what they thought might be the major reasons why women sometimes fail as leaders and it shocked me to learn that almost every lady I spoke to mentioned an issue of alias: PHD – in other words, 'pull her down.'

One would think that the era of women pulling each other down and bad mouthing each other were gone, wouldn't you?

Some years ago, I was preaching and while speaking at this particular conference, a particular lady whom I had never met before kept looking at me with much contempt all the time I was speaking from the podium. For a moment I was distracted by her antics but after a while, I chose to ignore her. Later I found out that she had been on a one woman campaign to have me barred from speaking at that conference. Funny thing was, I never knew her. I had never met nor spoken to her in my life but for one reason or the other she had decided that she didn't like me … or my guts.

In today's world, it is very common to see leading ladies openly stabbing other women in the back, all for the sake of dragging resources from a sister and increasing their own followership. Envy and jealousy have become the game and the order of the day, so a woman who does not play the game is often labelled proud and haughty.

When one leading lady continues to pull other leading ladies down, it can mean only one thing, she does not understand that, as the popular saying goes, putting out someone else's candle never makes yours shine brighter.

As an upcoming or even mature and experienced leading lady, you learn to live with these behaviours and, as I mentioned previously, you must dust yourself down, know who you are, accept that envy and jealousy are REAL in your world. Envy and jealousy can happen but you don't have to react badly. Instead, laugh through life and laugh a lot; Be jovial and friendly and kind but please, don't ever allow that jealousy and envy crack you open.

Life does happen!

When a leading lady does not have a mentor

Every leading lady needs a mentor and it is often said that we should not trust a mentor who has no mentor.

1 Corinthians 4:
'15 For though ye have ten thousand instructors in Christ yet have ye not many fathers: for in Christ Jesus, I have begotten you through the gospel.'

'3 Likewise, teach the older women to be reverent in the way they live, not to be slanderers or addicted to much wine, but to teach what is good. 4 Then they can urge the younger women to love their husbands and children, 5 to be self-controlled and pure, to be busy at home, to be kind, and to be subject to their husbands, so that no one will malign the word of God.'
Titus 2: 3-5

Often, when people look for mentors, they are looking for someone who would be partial in advice and guidance but that is actually the opposite of what a mentor is and what they do. Your mentors should be impartial and, being that usually they are more experienced in life and matters relating to your industry, they ought to be trusted and respected.

When a leading lady meets a good mentor, they will be motivated to be proactive and aspire to higher behaviours.

Advantages of having a mentor as a leading lady

1. You have someone to share your experiences with
2. You won't get lost easily at the crossroads
3. You will avoid costly mistakes
4. Your friends will most likely not tell you the truth about yourself or your journey but your mentor will always tell you the truth and that will enable you to make necessary life adjustments
5. You will get the privilege of new insights and fresh perspectives
6. You get an accountability partner
7. You remain in a learning environment and continue to learn and grow
8. No man or woman is an Island
9. It always takes two to tango
10. To achieve the impossible, you need people and you need support
11. When life throws challenges and storms at you, your mentor can help because they have been down that same route before
12. You need a non-judgemental critic who sees purpose, destiny and a bright future for you and they want to do everything possible to ensure that your vision does not die
13. You need a mentor to enable your strategic planning
14. Everyone needs an encourager not a dream killer

I must say, that as much as mentors are required, you are not allowed to stay in a toxic mentoring relationship. If you find yourself in one, get out because it is far better to live without one that live with that toxicity.

Leadership can be a lonely road

Another reason why leading ladies sometimes fail is because they have not understood that sometimes, they must run alone for a while, even while other women watch from a distance with a *let's see if she can make it* attitude.

So, some of us misunderstand that the *let's watch* attitude only usually lasts for a little while but we often take it as an insult to our ability to hit targets or pursue our God given goals. That can cause most to stop and no longer pursue their vision.

They say failure is an orphan but success has a large family, so a wise leading lady continues to run until she sees success. She continues to run until she finds her tribe and then, all those who thought she was a nobody who would never achieve her goals, will start to align themselves with her and desire to be a part of what God is helping her achieve.

CHAPTER FOUR

THE LEADING LADY
AND HER INFLUENCE

WHAT IS INFLUENCE?

At this point, it's time to look at the subject of influence. We have started to look at the leading lady and some of her characteristics but now let's pause and dig deeper into the word 'influence'.

As is my custom, here I will look into the various perspectives of a word or text.

Influence – 'The capacity to have an effect on the character, development or behaviour of someone'

The greatest influencer I know is Jesus Christ of Nazareth. It has been two thousand years after his death and yet, millions still love and follow Him. He changed our lives positively and he is not only a transformational influencer, but a social and heart influencer also and the list goes on.

It is very sad that so many people do not realise that leadership is influence – they go hand in hand. We cannot lead without having Influence in mind.

Just like treasure hunters when leaders meet someone who has hidden treasure inside of them that needs unlocking so they dedicate their time and wisdom to ensure those treasures are not only found but utilised. In a funny way, every one of us is an influencer and we unintentionally influence whether that is for good or bad. Our focus in this book is all about being a positive influence.

So, influential women are:

HELPERS: They are destiny helpers who give their mentees and protégé's the guidelines and support from their own life experience. I feel so much joy when I have heard from young men and women about how my life and determination has influenced them positively. That is such a blessing.

When I hear "thank you ma for teaching me to pray," I feel so much gratitude and a deep appreciation.

CONFIDENT IN THE LORD: No one can help another person if they themselves are groping around in the dark without knowing where they are going. So, we need to build confidence in God and skills for our development .

A leading lady needs to draw her confidence from God's wonderful words. And as leading ladies, we all face challenges that may shake our foundations but in those times, a wise woman runs to the word of God to regain her self-confidence and get back up on her feet.

Personally, I have a litmus test for my own confidence level and whenever I begin to develop a low self-esteem, I know I am not reading my bible as much as I should. In those times, I shut myself in to hear the word of God through the bible.

It is only from a place of confidence that we can mentor and influence others positively.

A confident woman is a woman on a journey to wholeness and as she seeks this, she is in a place where she does not throw trash at others. 'Hurt people hurt people' is a very old but true saying. Those who have been pained often inflict pain on others and that is why we must seek peace and confidence through God's word.

2 Corinthians 7: 16 (KJV)

'I rejoice therefore that I have confidence in you in all things.'

She is on a mission to change people's thinking, focus and patterns

Success, we have heard starts in the mind. Usually, we cannot conceive what we haven't thought about and, perhaps, this is the major doorway to influence. A leading lady can help others change the way they think about themselves and how they judge their own abilities.

When we started a branch of Triumphant Church International, in Port Harcourt, Nigeria, we had a good number of non-university graduates who loved God very much but did not have anyone to encourage them to go back to school. Of course, you must be aware that in Nigeria, it is at least a first degree from any university that would be required for a basic level of success or, to have any kind of status, as this is very important in the Nigerian culture.

As their Pastors, we decided that we would help them one at a time and help push them into their identity in Christ, so that they could take confident leaps into their destiny. One by one we began to give them support and encouragement and today, some of those students are the most committed financial members of that Church. What we did was teach them to see themselves the way God saw them and then, to walk in the knowledge of that new image.

One key ingredient of influence is helping people see themselves in their great future, not in their temporary today. Therefore, true influencers are constantly changing the opinions and behaviours of others into a positive mindset.

As the founder and vision bearer for 'The Wise Women Awards' www. wisewomenawards, I am always encouraging women to attend the awards so that they can hear other women's stories that will help them change their perspective to life, social justice, and community transformation.

When we host conferences and seminars or teach and mentor, our focus as women of influence, should be to ensure we guide their way of thinking to help them think more strategically, more focussed and more posterity oriented. In fact, more bible based and Jesus focused.

Women of influence are relevant to their world but let me add, that it must start from their Judea, then Samaria and after to Jerusalem then to the uttermost parts of the world. In simple terms, this means that this should start at home to influence our children and nuclear family, then take that influence out into the world.

WOMEN OF INFLUENCE GIVE BACK TO THEIR WORLD.

Giving back is mostly misconstrued and often limited to doing charitable work but it does go far beyond that and I believe that charitable work is good and must be done judiciously. If there was a term for it, I'd say I was a charity queen. I love and believe in charitable activities and most of my personal income goes into charitable work. As a church, we boldly state that you must give an umbrella to someone who is wet from the rain before you give them a bible tract.

We are very innovative with regards to charity work and each year, there are new ways in which we seek to reach out and support our community, in all our churches. We also never forget to remind ourselves that Jesus is the centre of whatever good we do.

Colossians 3:17, KJV: 'And whatsoever ye **do** in word or deed, **do** all in the **name of the Lord Jesus**, giving thanks to **God** and the Father by Him.'

Like I said, giving back goes far beyond any feeding or clothing project.

Mentors are giving back, coaches are giving back, volunteers are giving back, Pastors and other ministry gifts are giving back and teachers etc are giving back.

Matthew 26: 11

'For ye have the poor always with you; but me ye have not always.'

So, here's to charity, mentoring and coaching and as we give back, we must also seek avenues for developing others and *giving them a platform to exercise their gifts and talents.* That is a good definition of giving back. Often, people are reluctant to give back in this way because of how it has turned out in the past when people they helped became disloyal and ungrateful. EVEN JESUS was betrayed! So why bother? Just keep helping others. Keep inspiring them, keep giving back and influencing your world, one person at a time.

Charitable ventures can be very draining, both mentally and financially but it's always a joy to see the faces of those being helped, no matter how minute or small the help is. To think that someone would go to bed, breathe and thank God for your helping hand makes such a huge difference.

Women of influence are women who not only spot the gifts and talents of others but motivate them and get them to the place where they can fulfil their destiny. Personally, I am very intentional about my mentoring and guiding people on the path of purpose. Some of them you have to pamper, some you push, some need a subtle hand of push and some you must push to the platform by force. I do whatever is right for the person concerned.

I remember at the twentieth anniversary celebration of our church, my husband and I were so shocked at the number of people, preachers, music ministers etc. who said 'thank you Pastors Clem and Marjorie, you were the first to open a platform for me.'

Hey, wait for this - we would be lying if we said that some people, we helped didn't kick us on the face eventually. Some did kick us and they kicked hard but that didn't stop us from giving support and platform to others and never will it. We will always continue to give back.

The thing is some people will turn on you and that is just how life is. There was a lady I knew once who was terribly ill but she had no GP, so I begged mine to help her. Some years later, when we stopped going to the same church, she saw me as her enemy and out of the blue, a cab driver I knew called me to say this lady and her friend were talking about me in his cab and he swore that if he didn't know me himself, he would have thought they were talking about the Devil.

None of this affect us or our morals and intentions. I myself have opened an international ministry platform for people who later turned back and kicked me so hard, that I almost fell but by the power and encouragement of the Holy Spirit and the support of this Great Man of God, Pastor Clem, the husband of my youth, I pushed myself back up again. *Honey, thank you so very much.*

Let me repeat this - Influence is also about noticing the gifts and talents in others and supporting them to the best of our ability.

Followership is a by-product of Influence

Here I am reminded of the story of Mary and Martha, two sisters who followed and served our Lord Jesus Christ. (Luke 10 38-42)

Read JOHN 11: 19, 20, 28,29,31. When Martha rose up to meet with Jesus Christ she had walked alone to meet him and practically left unnoticed. When Mary rose up to meet him however, the women rose up with her and accompanied her on the journey. You see, influence brings about followership and our lives can have no genuine influence on others without a commitment to stay in the word of God and, in prayers at the feet of our Lord Jesus Christ. That is the example that Mary showed to us here and we can see the results. She didn't struggle or try to force a crowd. Her genuine influence and followership is a bona fide reward of following Christ.

There is a Chinese proverb that says, any leader who is leading without a following is practically just taking a walk.

So, what was the difference between Mary and Martha? Well, Mary always sat at the presence of the Lord and chose the 'better part', as Jesus had said. Any Christian leading lady who wants to influence others positively, must be a woman who spends time in God's presence, studying the word of God, praying and constantly worshipping.

Leadership is nothing without influence and I am grateful when many times, Pastors have told me thank you because, in their words, 'since my wife met you, her life changed and her attitude towards me and our ministry has changed positively.' Please understand that leadership is the ability to influence another person in heart and life matters and, the ability to change them for good to the glory of the Lord.

Many times, I have heard the words below or those similar to them, from ladies who have crossed my path -

'Pastor Marjorie, if you never give me any gift in life, I will still be forever grateful that you taught my family and I to pray'.

It is comments like this, that make me want to carry on and lead as I do.

iLead iChange iInfluence Mentoring Program

For several years we have undertaken mentoring for women in ministry, business and marriage etc. We have worked with women to bring them to a place where they can use their gifts from under the bushel (Matthew 5:15) and display them to the glory of the Lord for the benefit of their world and their community.

At the time of writing, we currently run a twelve week, three tier mentoring program called 'iLead, iChange and iInfluence,' for women in Ministry and leadership, plus any other woman who aspires to become a. great leader.

If you are interested in this programme and want to know more about this multilevel mentoring project, please email us at admin@ wisdomforwomeninternational.org

We would be very happy to work you through the program and into a place of significance.

How can you position yourself for a greater sphere of influence?

There is no doubt that everyone prays to live a life of influence and significance and so, we need to position ourselves so that we can live this life. At this stage, I must mention that the art of influence can be learnt, just as most leadership skills can.

Power is also important for leadership but as awesome as power is, influence is more important. Our influence will help us get ahead in situations where there are no clear-cut rules on an issue. That's why influence really has little to do with titles and positions.

Never think to influence any person or organisation on a short term basis. Always think long term and always think of influence from a sustainable basis.

So, how do you position yourself for greater influence?

1. Networking

Networking is a craft that can be learned and you can read more about this in Chapter five. Undoubtedly, strategic Networking will position you for influence and success.

2. Stay credible

Mentees and protegees are always looking for credibility and also for people with a genuine interest in their lives and affairs

3. Technology and social media

Today, most key influencers are the people who are making an impact in the world through social media and through this modality, they are able to persuade, inform and inspire with their various posts and comments.

4. **Expertise**

When we are experts in our sphere of influence, we can influence the opinion of others.

5. **Give Back**

- Kindness leadership
- Use the power of appeal and persuasion
- Use the art of mobilisation
- Use the skills of collaboration

CHAPTER FIVE

· · · · · · · · · · · ❖ · · · · · · · · · · · ·

INGREDIENTS FOR TWENTY FIRST CENTURY LEADERSHIP

More and more women have risen to the forefront of leadership in different spheres of life in this century, in recent years. The political scene has seen an increase of top national female leaders with a good handful of Presidents and Prime Ministers among them.

Incidentally, I recently read a review and comparison on the corona virus outbreak with its spread and fatalities in various nations of the world and I noticed that the majority of countries where the virus had the most minimum impact, were countries that were being led by women (as at August 2020), e.g., Germany, Denmark, Finland, Iceland, New Zealand, Slovakia, Norway and Taiwan. These countries have been said to handle the Covid 19 crisis more effectively than other countries that are being managed by male counterparts.

If you asked me why these leaders have ensured that their countries faired successfully during the pandemic, I would be tempted to talk about emotional intelligence, authenticity and the panoramic view of women in general, when put in charge of a crises, challenge or problem to solve.

Leadership for women in this century comes with its own peculiar challenges, especially for those in any sector that has a masculine focus. The church is one key area where, for generations, the men have had the front row seat but in the twenty first century, the women have gradually emerged from the shadows and are slowly picking up their voices. Christian women in leadership, in this century, have seen both many positive and negative turns.

We will look at the many positives here and perhaps, glean through a few of the negatives.

Transformational leadership

Lately, We have seen a push towards transformational leadership by women and they have risen up in this generation as mentors, coaches, social advocates, entrepreneurs and serial entrepreneurs, to name just a few.

We have also seen the emergence of many networking and accountability groups that have been formed and led by women with most of these having the focus of teamwork and mobilisation.

The power of networking and collaboration

Women are natural collaborators and networkers and repeatedly, we have seen this tendency grow as women learn to put away their differences and any negative feelings of 'crabology' (the pull her down (PHD) syndrome), in order to link up with other likeminded women and organisations so that together, they can further their dreams and aspirations..

Here I'll explain a quick and basic differentiation between networking and collaboration and I have to say, women do both very well.

Networking is usually based on trust and it's not always a formal relationship but mostly informal, with an intention to come together to work and advance a project or purpose.

Organisations can come together intentionally and non-intentionally, which they do to network with the purpose of working together and moving a project forward, as I mentioned above. This is based on trust.

But a Collaboration usually has a stronger tie, although it is mostly limited to two or more organisations, when they come together for the purpose of achieving the advancement of a project or cause.

If your organisation were to collaborate with another, then you **MUST** put a simple contract in place and if that is not possible, at least discuss, at length, the terms of the collaboration.

When we started 'The Wise Women Awards', we operated at a basic level until we collaborated with other organisations, like 'Keep The Faith' magazine and other major sponsors. That collaboration so greatly enhanced the profile of Wisdom For Women International and The Wise Women Awards to a capacity of more than one hundred percent by the first year of collaboration.

So, collaboration and networking are key strategies that have come to the frontline and been used as success factors by leading ladies in this century. However, a leading lady will take time to seek the face of God before any collaboration or networking is pursued.

You know, some time ago, I realised that many who request collaboration are actually smooth operators whose behaviour is more like that of a car on a ram raid. The only reason they come close to you is because they want to break into your network.

However, I would also say that despite some of the downsides of collaboration, it is still the way to go. It is the Elizabeth and Mary thing and it is the Naomi and Ruth thing.

'41 When Elizabeth heard Mary's greeting, the baby leaped in her womb, and Elizabeth was filled with the Holy Spirit. 42 In a loud voice she exclaimed: "Blessed are you among women and blessed is the child you will bear!' Luke 1: 41 – 42 (NIV)

Collaborate with others only when the metaphorical baby in your womb leaps when you see them, otherwise, please stay away and protect your assignment from ram raiders and destiny spoilers. Better still, even if they don't fall into either of those categories, they just may not be for you at the time. Do always keep them in mind for the future maybe as you might connect better then, but for now, please stay on your own lane.

Now, when you find the right collaborative team or partners It is important that you stick through it all to see the full realisation of that collaboration. Relationships, whether personal or organisational will always be tested, so it is important that you do your utmost to define the terms of the collaboration and that way, hopefully it will pass any test of strain.

Collaborations and Networking do not necessarily have to be upwards but can be with peers and even downwards, just so long as you are clear about what mutual benefits you wish to accomplish between you.

Pastor Marjorie's personal rules for Networking and Collaborations

1. I don't need everyone. Go for those you know you can develop a mutually beneficial relationship with.
2. Don't ask for favours. You offer support first.
3. Never cross moral lines. Do everything possible to keep your integrity intact
4. If, every time you speak to me, you keep looking over my shoulder for someone else, that's it, you don't value me and I don't have time for you either. Doesn't sound Christian I guess but sorry, in some matters you cannot afford to be emotional. These are matters of destiny and we cannot play around with them.
5. Be yourself. Don't force anything. Don't force any relationship.

Develop Your Personal Brand

Branding became a word we heard regularly during this century. All leading women were constantly reminded of the need to develop and upgrade their brands and here, I would like to simplify and demystify the issue of branding as indeed, it is crucial that the leading lady develops her brand.

Let me start with what a brand is not, as most have confused brand assets with branding.

Please note that as much as all of these are important, they are not your brand. We will get to what it is soon

Your brand is *not* your logo, your icon, your slogan, your organisations colours or your name.

Dear Leading Lady, what then is your brand?

- ❑ It's what you stand for in other people's minds i.e., your clients, members etc.
- ❑ The experience you give people in the short and long term
- ❑ The understanding of why you exist as a business/brand.
- ❑ Your organisational and life's mission and purpose
- ❑ And the day-to-day operational strategies of how you accomplish your goals

You can see that all the above are linked to matters of integrity and relationship i.e., how you operate and deal with others.

That is the reason why leaders fall when, despite everything, the PR and things like budget, open a gap in integrity. You can spend all your money on marketing and image consultancy but still fall if your integrity slips.

A leading lady therefore, must never forget that she is *the brand,* not the flyers, images or marketing but the values she possesses personally, which she is able to infuse into her organisation.

With Wisdom For Women International, one of the vows we made was that no one would ever leave any of our events and bite their tongues for feeling cheated or short changed. We have infused that and many other values throughout our organisational brand and the day we fall short in that, no matter the publicity or marketing, we will already have left a bad taste in the mouth of people who attended one or more of our many events.

We vowed to always make people feel like they got so much more than they paid for at any of our events that they attended.

Now that we have seen the core ingredients of a leading ladies brand, which is her ethics and integrity, we can now take a quick look at some other things that she can do to upgrade her brand.

The pictures and images that we throw around social media go a long way to speak about us as people. The leading lady needs to dress and speak in a way that would not bring any reproach to the body of Christ, whom she represents. When people take selfies with me, I always ask to look before they post them. Someone might say that is self-worship or self-glorification but it isn't. What I want is to represent Christ well in the public eye. We must have standards in our dressing and there really should be some kind of difference between the church and the outside world.

A Twenty First Century Leading lady should.

1. Wear their strength and dignity as clothing. This is an indication that your dress sense forms a part of your assets and reflects on who you are. It is not a façade to hide behind or hide the insecurities, fears or strengths that the lady is dealing with at that moment. What it is a show of trust in God. It is the leading lady laughing without a fear of the future

'She is clothed with strength and dignity,
and she laughs without fear of the future'. Proverbs 31: 25 (NLT)

2. A leading lady must dress with discretion and always listen to what her heart says as she dresses for the day.

'A beautiful woman who lacks discretion
is like a gold ring in a pig's snout'. Proverbs 11: 22 (NLT)

3. In modest and appropriate dressing which means it has to suit the occasion you are attending.

'And I want women to be modest in their appearance.[a] *They should wear decent and appropriate clothing and not draw attention to themselves by the way they fix their hair or by wearing gold or pearls or expensive clothes'.* 1 Timothy 2: 9 (NLT)

Press pictures

I would recommend that annually, you have some professional pictures taken and this should be part of your budget for each year. I actually smiled for a second as I wrote this bit and wondering why some leading ladies in the so called third world will send a good press picture when asked for it? I know how many times we have had to go back and forth for pictures to publicise the winners at the UK & European version of The Wise Women Awards. Many times it has been so exasperating and frustrating. But, if you ask their West African counterparts for their press pictures we are always slightly shocked at the great quality pictures they send and the speed with which they send them. It is like they are always ready for that moment.

As we are still talking about branding, it is important that your photographs and videos say exactly what you want people to know about you. No one can tell your story better than you can.

Dear leading lady, occasionally it is okay to scroll down your social media feeds, read through and make sure that your posts and photographs are saying and showing you just the way you want them to.

In summary, your brand is formed and determined by your actions and your activities. Your actions are more important than your logo, website, flyers, pictures or any publicity materials because, you, your person and your image are the brand and, as Aristotle said, *"The soul never thinks without an image."*

In actual fact, what we do is speak so loud that people can't possibly hear what we are saying. Actions speak louder than words remember.

In conclusion, you are the most valuable asset of your organisation. You are the brand and as such you must carry and hold yourself in that value.

Don't forget, every day you are creating your brand and for every post you put on social media, you are further creating your brand.

"A good name is rather to be chosen than great riches, and loving favour rather than silver and gold" Proverbs 22:1 KJV

CHAPTER SIX

· · · · · · · · · · · ❖ · · · · · · · · · · ·

THE LEADING LADY AND CULTURAL INTELLIGENCE

In a book like this it would not feel right if I didn't look at the topic of cultural intelligence. In previous years, we have heard discussions about intelligence quotient but, in recent years, we are starting to learn that, to lead effectively, a lady must be culturally diverse and culturally aware. With the level of racial hate, we see in our world today, it is crucial that this becomes a topic for all leading ladies.

So, what is cultural Intelligence and why do we need to talk about it?

1. *Possessing the ability to work across various cultures.* A leading lady cannot achieve much without an ability to spread across different cultures. When you know that your dream is bigger than people of your race, culture, age and financial status, you will seek to create an environment around you that accommodates people from all cultures.

2. *Possessing the ability to function effectively within different cultural contexts.* I will explain this in more detail as we explore the principle of culture. That is because culture goes beyond race, dress and language and it takes a level of discipline and strategic planning to be able to manoeuvre within a diverse cultural setting.

At all the Wisdom for Women International meetings, we consciously create an atmosphere that will accommodate people from different races and age ranges and so, in most of our conferences such as the Wise Women Awards and the Wise Women Pray, we have been able to record close to a number of not less than twenty different nations who are being represented in attendance.

3. *To have responsible global citizenship.* I have sat with many leading ladies who would put aside all care and consideration for others in their midst, simply to converse in their native tongue. In these cases, what they do not understand is that, even without speaking or complaining, they have excluded someone who they could have provided a positive influence to.

As a speaker, I consider myself an international citizen, as doors have opened for me across nations and cultures, therefore, with serious intent, I respect my global citizenship and the people around me who are often of a different culture.

4. *The Ability to understand and be tutored in different cultural perspective.* Many people from different cultures will naturally see things from a different perspective to us. Sadly, growing up, our parents transferred their suspicions of other countries, tribes and cultures to us and, personally, as I grew, I began to unlearn some of the things I had been told about other people and their cultures. A combination of sociability and solidarity is what makes up a culture and these two features help us to understand the ethos of certain groups we belong to or associate with. All cultures do things differently and as a leading lady you need to acquire the ability to see people from the culture they belong to. Those skills help us navigate and negotiate our way through to the way of success that is why understanding culture is very important from a leading lady's perspective. Relating to people from other cultures is a key skill for a leading lady.

If you want to reach your goals and aspirations, then you must learn about people and cultures who are different from you. I would recommend that you regularly scroll through the names in your phone and ascertain what the dominant age group, language, race, colour and profession is and, if you find any gaps, please fill them by intentional strategy.

<u>What is culture</u>

I used to think that culture was merely about someone's way of life perspective, race, colour and language. Certainly, it is about a way of life but it is also so much more than race, colour and language.

Every group of people have their own lifestyle, have a culture and so, there are cultures that are determined by age and sex differences and not just race or language e.g.

- Youth culture
- Teenage culture
- Childhood culture
- Senior citizen's culture
- Women's culture
- Men's culture

The list goes on.

Different races have different ways of life and therefore, a different culture. The same applies to people of different nations.

Different genders, have a different way of life and so, a different culture. Singles, couples, different gender identification, different religions and so on and so forth.

Dear leading lady, I have gone through the list above to emphasise the need for us all to have a plan for focussing our goals and aspirations so that we can influence beyond our own culture.

When we have this insight, we can expand our influence through any cultural barriers that may have existed because we didn't understand the vastness of culture. So, as a ministry we would host programmes like mother and daughter days to incorporate the younger generation and to introduce them to our world and therefore, our culture.

We are learning each and every day and each day gives us the opportunity to learn more about cultural values, which we must know if we want to cut across the board. Life is a learning curve, as is travelling. A leading lady should travel with the intention to learn from other cultures, no matter whether they are travelling for leisure, speaking engagements or business. There are many of us who have committed cultural blunders and bloopers and it happens without intention.

I remember coming to join my husband from Nigeria to the UK as he had been called into ministry to serve the UK. I had done some work in the city, temping with various companies and one of the first was a mortgage finance company in South West London. I observed during my time there that people took it in turns to serve tea, and on this particular day, it was the Chief Executive who came to ask if I wanted tea. In Nigeria, where I was coming from as a General Manager of a Finance company, there would be no circumstances where the boss would serve tea to anyone. That would be unheard of.

So, when the CEO came to ask if I wanted some tea, I declined and said I didn't feel like a cup of tea, even though I desperately wanted one. In my little mind I was not ready to loose my job!

Here is a good place to share some quick strategies for living a consistent culturally aware lifestyle.

1. Remember that you need more than the Intelligence Quotient IQ
2. Decide to be intentional about cross cultural matters.
3. Learn to be flexible with things that don't really matter, e.g., food, dress etc.
4. Accept and understand what your core values are and be flexible with other issues. For me matters of faith, integrity and excellence

are my core values and with those, culture does not override them but exists outside of them. I am very willing to be flexible and am happy to learn songs from other cultures and adopt different eating styles and food.

5. You must recognise that not everyone is like you. Others won't necessarily speak the same as you nor will they have same the principles and values you do – shouting and telling people they have an accent for instance would be indecent. It would not be good if everyone around looked and talked exactly like you.

6. Be curious about other cultures and do engage and participate with people from them cultures.

7. Form strong and lasting relationships with people from other cultures

What are the faces of culture that we should be aware of?

Language is a key cultural face. There are many different languages to ours but that does not make those people different from us. Language gives a group of people an identity; an individuality that they require, perhaps even crave for within a multidimensional society. As much as language enhances our identity, it can also be a strong dividing factor for even the smallest of groups. That is why members of a local church or group have to be sensible and not speak in a language that is not universal or this will be to the detriment of the group or church. That is why many churches have emerged as a one tribe or one culture church.

This tells me that if I need to minister to the youth, I must learn about their language so that I can reach them. So that I can communicate effectively with them.

Another face of culture is body language and this means different things for different cultures. A leading lady must make conscious efforts to understand the culture of others. People have body language and those actions can mean different things to different cultures. When we understand that, we tend to be less judgemental about others. Raised as an African and a Nigerian in particular, this means that when I am speaking to my elders,

I am expected not to look at their eyes but lower my eyes to the floor. For someone who does not know this, they may come to the UK and make this very mistake while talking to an elder, their boss or someone in authority and this would be looked upon as lack of confidence or as timidity.

The list of the faces of culture continues e.g., the values systems, the idioms, food, dress and dances etc. It is therefore very important to ask why people do what they do. The safest way to go about this is to ask questions before we make any judgements and, to always make a quick assessment of what is major and what is minor to you, as a leading lady in Christ. For me, I repeat the bible overrides culture but for other minor matters, I am willing to be flexible to accommodate others, so long as it's not a hell or heaven matter.

A leading lady must then look at a group of people from the perspective of their stories, myths, their rituals, symbols and their power structures etc. so as to understand their culture.

CHAPTER SEVEN

. . . . ❖ . . . .

THE LEADING LADY
AND HER WISDOM

A leading lady needs to understand the importance of wisdom in her role.

Without wisdom she cannot be effective in her service to God and to man. Wisdom is what takes a leading lady beyond charisma. Charisma is able to take us to new dimensions but wisdom is what distinguishes one season from the other for a leading lady.

1. HOW CAN WE DEFINE WISDOM?

The bible defines wisdom as 'the Principal thing' (Proverbs 4:7). Principal means it is the most important thing a leading lady requires to enable her do ministry, pursue a career, run a business, be a wife, a mother and a woman of influence.

In this world of rat race in women's ministry and women empowerment, it is almost scary (speaking from my own viewpoint) to do anything without seeking God so the leading lady would truly need to depend on God for Godly wisdom. (James 3: 17)

We would require wisdom in discerning:

'A wise heart to help us discern good from evil' (Hebrews 5:14)

46

Without a wise heart, how else can we achieve maximum output from the few resources we have available? How else can we know who should be on our team and who should not? How could we have the heart to know which projects to run and which ideas to dump? And the heart to know what should be on our year planner and what shouldn't be. I am currently writing in the pandemic of covid 19 era and seeing how this pandemic has hit us so suddenly I'm discerning that life would not be the same again post pandemic. We need the spirit of wisdom to navigate the future that is ahead of us.

Wisdom demands we take cautious steps that are balanced with faith. And so, there is need to watch the economic, social and religious climate and then take decisive steps as we walk these curvy and uncertain terrains as leading ladies. This is not the time to copy or dare I say, jump and copy what others are doing but a time to seek God and hear Him for yourself.

In these turbulent and uncertain days, a leading lady must take decisive steps that are prayed over to emerge as a reinvention from the old. Changes and adjustments must be made to take the bold steps that are required to conquer the unknown and any uncertain scenarios that may present themselves during the pandemic and after it.

2. Wisdom is a Spirit

There are several verses that point us to thirst for wisdom and that wisdom a leading lady seeks is from above. There is a clear difference between being worldly wise and the wisdom that comes from God. We need the spirit of Godly wisdom to help us make decisions as career women, wives, businesswomen, ministers of the gospel and parents etc.

'But the wisdom from above is first of all pure. It is also peace loving, gentle always, and willing to yield to others. It is full of mercy and the fruit of good deeds. It shows no favouritism and is always sincere." James 3: 17 NLT

Let us see some manifestation of Godly wisdom from the scripture.

'And thou shalt speak unto all that are wise hearted, whom I have filled with the spirit of wisdom, that they may make Aaron's garments to consecrate him, that he may minister unto me in the priest's office.' Exodus 28: 3 KJV

Here, God assigned those with the spirit of wisdom to make the priestly garments for consecration. This was a great assignment because, as you will recollect, no Priest was allowed to go before God in just any attire. They had to dress in the appropriate clothing as specified by God.

'And Joshua the son of Nun was full of the spirit of wisdom; for Moses had laid his hands upon him: and the children of Israel hearkened unto him and did as the LORD commanded Moses. Deuteronomy.' 34: 9

Above is more evidence of the power in the spirit of wisdom. No wonder Joshua accomplished all that he did as a leader in Israel, leading the Israelites safely to the promised land. Joshua 1: 24 indicates that it was he who led the Israelites into Canaan. Remember, he needed the wisdom of God to deal with all the battles on the way to the promised land.

My prayer is that you and I be full of the spirit of wisdom. Amen.

Growing up as a believer in Christ, this admonition from Apostle Paul to the Church in Ephesus, was one of the first that I learned. A leader in today's world, without the spirit of wisdom and revelations, will truly be limited in making right choices, in cutting edge advancement, in dealing with crises moments and understanding seasons. There are issues that come before you as a leading lady in ministry, marriage, parenting, or your business, right there at the board meeting table and they require instant solutions. In those situations, you will need the spirit of wisdom.

'[I always pray] that the God of our Lord Jesus Christ, the Father of glory, may grant you a spirit of wisdom and of revelation [that gives you a deep and personal and intimate insight] into the true knowledge of Him [for we know the Father through the Son].' Ephesians 1: 17 AMP

Now you understand why Solomon says:

"Wisdom is the principal thing; therefore get wisdom: and with all thy getting get understanding". Proverbs 4: 7 KJV

The first and foremost desire of a leading lady is to walk and operate in the wisdom of the Lord, so as not to crash. So as not to plateau in destiny and to stay relevant till the end of her course. So, we can truly say, 'She served her generation well.' (Acts 13: 36). And you, as a leading lady, can truly say "I walked in the mind of God. I strategised in God's power and not mine,' and so, you can truly say that you operated in divine strategy to overcome rather than your own power.

This spirit of wisdom gives us the strategies for financial prosperity and financial prudence.

A question people often ask me is, *how do you finance all that you do, the events and the many projects?* My answer will always be *by divine wisdom* and that wisdom comes from above.

THE LEADING LADY'S DAILY PRAYER FOR DIVINE WISDOM

'If you need wisdom, ask our generous God, and he will give it to you. He will not rebuke you for asking.' James 1: 5 NLT

Lord, I cannot lead by myself, my knowledge and my insight is limited without you.

Lord, I pray for deep insight into God's word as I read and study the word of God.

Father fill my heart with thoughts that are pure, so that I may lead with Grace and godly wisdom. I pray like Solomon for the heart to discern good from evil.

Through the wisdom of God, may I have the ability and power to access great open doors and to walk in the wisdom that keeps those doors open for as long as he has ordained

Help me make decisions and choices purely to glorify you Lord and not for my own comfort and pride.

Lord Jesus, I submit my life to you and ask that you override and block all decisions and choices that I intend to make, outside of your will.

Guide me in your wisdom in all areas of my life, job, career, parenting, relationships, marriages, ministry and finance etc.

Lord bless me with the wisdom to judge things rightly, as in the spirit of Solomon and the two prostitutes. Let the power of errors and mistakes be broken over my life in Jesus mighty name.

The wisdom of God henceforth gives me the grace to avoid foolish mistakes, wrong associates, wrong collaborations and to walk in sync with God and never out of sync with the Lord.

Lord bless me with night dreams and open visions from the Holy Spirit each day that I might hear from you and you alone.

Father in Jesus mighty name, cut off all Ahitophelic instructors and keep those advisers away from me, my husband, my children and my children's children, my staff, associates and all who are close to me.'

In Jesus mighty name I pray. Amen.

THERE ARE FOUR WORDS USED FOR WISDOM IN THE BIBLE

CHOKMAH

The first word 'CHOKMAH', means to be experienced. This is the wisdom that comes from experience, e.g., David had fought the bear and the Lion and so he said he could also fight the Goliath the giant. Many of us do not like challenges but a multipurpose woman must realise that these build us up and make us know the Lord better. Romans tell us that *'challenges and problems create patience.'* (Romans 5: 3-5)

Chokmah is also the knowledge and the ability to make the right choices at the right time, based on life experiences.

Yes, it is okay to do the right thing but if it is done at the wrong time, then it can be classed as foolishness.

A multipurpose woman therefore, must always pray and ask the Lord for the grace to operate in God's right time. If we still do things at the wrong time, as Christians, we need to pray for the spirit of maturity, so that we can multitask.

- You wish to travel but is it the right time to do so?
- You need to change job but is now really the right time?
- Is it the right time to buy that car or should you use that money for land?
- You may be angry but is it the right time to speak about it?

WHAT WISDOM WILL DO FOR YOU?

'Long life, promotion, wealth, and length of days.' Prov 4: 5-9
'Substance, treasures'. Prov 8 Vs 21
'Long life and favour.' Prov 8 Vs 35-36
'Directions at the crossroad.' James 1: 5
'Give us an inheritance of glory.' Prov 3: 35

SEKEL

The word, SEKEL, is another word for wisdom, which means prudence (foresight and caution), intelligence, understanding and success. There can be no success without the wisdom of God. Remember that 'Wisdom comes from the fear of God.' Prov 9: 10

Another word for wisdom is Sophia

This means higher wisdom as it comes from above. Some people think they are wise because they are worldly wise but that is not wisdom from above. This makes them cunning, not wise. When someone has a broad knowledge of various things they possess Sophia. The ability to interpret dreams also comes to us when we possess this kind of wisdom. The ability to govern and administrate is also encompassed in this kind of wisdom and I am sure that you can now see why multipurpose and wisdom have to go hand in hand.

Another word for wisdom is phronesis

This is wisdom to deal with practical matters. Phronesis is important for us to operate as multipurpose women. There is no point saying that you are wise and then not be able to deal with everyday matters in your life and in the lives of those around you. When life overwhelms you dear leading lady, please pray for phronesis.

So, what are the practical ways to gain wisdom?

'How much better is it to get wisdom than gold! and to get understanding rather to be chosen than silver.' Proverbs 16: 16 KJV

The scriptures admonish the leading woman that she needs to GET wisdom. To get means to go after and obtain and that requires action and drive. Here are some practical ways we can get ourselves equipped for more godly wisdom.

'The fear of the Lord is the beginning of wisdom: and the knowledge of the holy is understanding.' Proverbs 9: 10 KJV

1. 'Ask for wisdom from the Lord.' James 1: 5
2. Seek God's face for wisdom
3. Read and study the bible as that is the source of pure ultimate wisdom
4. Read books from reputable and experienced authors
5. 'Follow the wise and become wiser.' Proverbs 13: 20
6. 'Stay away from the foolish as it leads to harm.' 13: 20
7. Seek avenues for self-development, even if you have to pay for yourself
8. Take training courses and continue to learn

9. Seek wise mentors
10. Have a coach
11. Get life Lessons from criticism
12. Get life Lessons from suffering
13. Always remember the golden rule. Treat others as you want to be treated.
14. 'Ask God to guide your sentences.' Psalm 17: 2

CHAPTER EIGHT

. . . . ❖ . . . .

THE LEADING LADY AND HER BALANCED LIFE

There is so much that beckons a leading lady daily. Some beckon us so strongly and others lightly with subtilty. A lot of women today wear many caps – that of a wife, mother, businesswoman, mentor, career woman, and for some, like me, Pastor. Of course, the list goes on.

The question of how a leading lady lives a balanced life, is an age old question that many have tried to answer. I personally would truly want to look at this from the bible perspective, tying it to our day-to-day struggles to balance life and to live stress free to the best of our abilities.

You will never have too much time to yourself. Even when we were home, locked down during the pandemic, we realised that we still did not have enough time to do all the things we wanted to do. Have you ever felt that you needed forty-eight hours or more in a day?

This is my daily prayer to the Lord,

'For length of days and long life
And peace they will add to you.' Proverbs 3: 2 NKJV

By now we know that God is not prodigal with words and never uses words that are not necessary, so we can easily tell that length of days and a long life would obviously mean two different things.

Wisdom therefore, gives us length of days which, in my understanding, is the ability to do a lot more than normal in a particular space of time. That is, the days becoming lengthened and the hours stretching supernaturally to enable us to achieve more and more each day.

This comes with unction that you receive from the Holy Spirit that which makes your workload easier and then you are able to tackle problems and challenges faster while completing more tasks quicker than normal.

'And her lamp does not go out by night.' Proverbs 31:15

'She also rises while it is yet night.' Proverbs 31:18

At this stage, may I please recommend that we take a pause and meditate on the life of the woman of Proverbs 31. For me, two verses stand out in that chapter - verses 15 and 18. She seems to be busy all day 24/7. Is that what is required of us as leading ladies? I would say 'no.'

What I see in Proverbs 31 is a woman who is a strategic planner, a delegator and a team player. A woman with a strong perception. I do not see a perfectionist here. That is why you should not read that chapter and work yourself up, getting stressed and creating a mental disorder because you want to be a Proverbs 31 woman.

Here I will list what has worked for me personally:

1. Every day has its own priority assignment as does every year and every month. I work on my priorities, as given to me by the Lord. Our priority, if determined by the Holy Spirit, means that we allow God to order our steps. When God does this, we become people whose lives are directed by the Spirit of God into pleasant places. Do daily only what you have unction for.

One evening I said to Pastor Clem, "You aren't writing much these days?" He casually replied, "I can only write when there is the unction and right now I have no unction"

When a leading lady stays in God's presence, early in the morning, she is able to get direction from the Holy Spirit for the day, which God Himself will enable her to accomplish.

Order my steps Lord Psalm 119: 133

2. Each day, year, and month releases a special grace and anointing to me. So, there are years when I write more, do certain events more, create new initiatives more and so it goes on. What I am saying is, as a leading lady, you must grow to a place of recognising the anointing for each day and walking into the grace and unction for each season. That is the way to work without stress and ensure that you are living the balanced life.

3. Always ask for the direction of the Holy Spirit because when the Holy Spirit leads us, he makes us do what's needful and required for each season. I have woken up on certain days and not done any work at all, as all I felt I wanted to do was go out and have fun, shopping, eating, and visiting places of interest. I would do this some days and not feel guilty at all. Why? Because that is the unction I had from the Holy Spirit and you know what? As I catch up with work the next day, I do it so fast that it's almost unbelievable.

4. Work with templates. Each year I will do around ten conferences and events within the umbrella of Wisdom for Women International. This is excluding church events and church services. It would be very irrational and almost unheard of, to reinvent the wheel each time we start a new programme or a new year. So, what do I do to work through these programmes without stress? I use templates for most things I do and I work with lists. I would not go on a major shopping time for my home without a list. I would not travel for ministry without a list. Things as basic as my face towel and bedroom slippers are all on that list, which helps me free up time for other things.

Every event has its own set template and we simply dust it off each year, upgrade it a little but retain the skeleton of it. That way, I don't reinvent the wheel each year.

5. Do not join the rat race! Life sometimes feels like a rat race as does Ministry but you must determine not to join it. The best and most Spirit filled way to achieve this is to not break rank. Stay on your own lane.

As a soldier of Christ, I have learned to stay on my own path and not change course. A leading lady who wants to live a balanced life will not easily change course, except when she hears expressly from God. Many today are bugged with stress, envy, jealousy and financial burden because they keep changing their course and breaking rank. That is how I have stayed fresh in my walk with God and the pursuit of my destiny and purpose. It has to be God or we throw it in the bin.

'They shall run like mighty men; they shall climb the wall like men of war; and they shall march everyone on his ways, and they shall not **break their ranks**' Joel 2: 7

'Like warriors they charge; like soldiers they climb the wall. Each keeps to their own path; they didn't change their course.' Joel 2: 7 (Common English Bible)

6. Live a planned and organised life.

If I was asked what was one of my favourite bible verses, Luke 14, would be in the top ten.

'But don't begin until you count the cost. For who would begin construction of a building without first calculating the cost to see if there is enough money to finish it?' Luke 14: 28 NLT

We need to live a life that is organised and planned. This verse does not necessarily refer to finance alone but to planning in general. Jesus tells us in John 14: 3 that He was going to prepare a place for us, so that one day we would be where He, our Saviour, is and live with Him for eternity. Listen that was over two thousand years ago. Wouldn't you have thought *Ooohhh that's Jesus Christ, so He could wave a wand and bang, our mansions would appear, all ready for check in?* But our Saviour chose to spend time, plan and implement the plan for our future home.

A leading lady must have a daily, weekly and monthly diary and an annual year planner. My year planner is always ready and ticked by the first week of December, in preparation for the next year. To an extent this year planner is followed strictly but sometimes, we are flexible if God overrides it.

We have also followed the pattern of putting in place, five-year plans for our work at Wisdom For Women International, which by the power of the Holy Spirit we always seem to have met our goals around ninety percent of the time. Not bad for a girl from downtown Port Harcourt, Nigeria.

Lord I am grateful.

7. Find your dominant gift and stay within it. The reason I say that is because other gifts will flow as multiple streams of income. One of my bible heroines is Deborah, who the scriptures describe as a Wife, Prophetess, Judge and a Warrior. Not forgetting, of course, she was a songwriter too.

'Deborah, the wife of Lappidoth, was a prophet who was judging Israel at that time. ⁵ She would sit under the Palm of Deborah, between Ramah and Bethel in the hill country of Ephraim, and the Israelites would go to her for judgment.' Judges 4: 4 – 5 NLT

Deborah is recorded as the only female Judge that Israel had at that time and it is interesting to note that her dominant gift was being a Prophet. Take note that all the other gifts flowed from that prophetic gift. Here was a woman of balance in that she didn't struggle to walk in any of her gifts. All the other expression of those gifts were prophetic, so all she was doing to succeed as a judge was to depend on that Prophetic gift to discern and judge right.

For her to win at that war, she stayed in her prophetic gift to know which battle to fight and she only went for the 'win win.'

"One day she sent for Barak son of Abinoam, who lived in Kedesh in the land of Naphtali. She said to him, *This is what the LORD, the God of Israel, commands you: Call out 10,000 warriors from the tribes of Naphtali and Zebulun at Mount Tabor. ⁷ And I will call out Sisera, commander of Jabin's army, along with his chariots and warriors, to the Kishon River. There I will give you victory over him.*" Judges 4: 6-7 NLT

That way there was no sweating and no stress whatsoever. She woke up every day and every day she was be a Prophetess. That was all she did and that is why I believe she could conveniently find her balance and flow as a wife, warrior, judge, prophet and also, write the prophetic song in chapter 5 of The Book Judges.

8.   As a leading lady, to live a balanced life, we need to do only that which God has ordained for us. No less and no more. When we do more, it becomes cumbersome and when we take on less, we are not utilising the full power of God upon our lives.

'Moses said to them, It is the bread the LORD has given you to eat. ¹⁶ This is what the LORD has commanded: Everyone is to gather as much as they need. Take an omer[a] for each person you have in your tent.

¹⁷ The Israelites did as they were told; some gathered much, some little. ¹⁸ And when they measured it by the omer, the one who gathered much did not have too much, and the one who gathered little did not have too little. Everyone had gathered just as much as they needed.

¹⁹ Then Moses said to them, *No one is to keep any of it until morning.*

²⁰ However, some of them paid no attention to Moses; they kept part of it until morning, but it was full of maggots and began to smell. So, Moses was angry with them.'

Exodus 16: 16-20

The story above shows us that God's instructed the children of Israel, not to take more than He had allotted to them but when they disobeyed, maggots grew into their supply of the manna. That is how we become overwhelmed with despair and stress, when we take on more than God has ordained for us.

10:

Live a life of Grace. What is Grace? Grace is enablement and power to DO. Grace is a gift we receive from the Lord.

"For by grace are ye saved through faith; and that not of yourselves: it is the gift of God" Ephesians 2: 8

It is the grace of God that carries us through trials and temptations. It is the grace of God that makes a leading woman wear all the caps she must wear and does not sweat the small stuff. She still carries herself with poise and dignity. She does not cave in because she gets her strength and enablement for her assignment from on high.

Grace is so powerful that, although it cannot be touched, it is intense. 2 Peter 1: 2 and 2 Peter 3: 18 both make us understand that the grace of God upon our lives has the possibility to grow, as we read and study the word of God. I have often advised leading ladies that as we grow in ministry and leadership, one very important ingredient we require is Grace. So, we must grow in the study of God's word so that we can increase in grace and enablement for ministry. No one can live the balanced life without the grace of God upon their lives. My prayer for you is that the grace of the Lord will increase more and more in your life and ministry.

CHAPTER NINE

. . . . ❖ . . . .

THE LEADING LADY, HER WARFARE, PRAYER AND INTERCESSION

One of the views I constantly project is that no one can be bigger than their private prayer life. The world of a leading lady is busy but as a man of God once said, I am so busy today that I have to pray more today. It means that the busier we are, the more we must pay attention to our prayer life. Prayer is more important than the very air that a Christian woman breathes.

To live a life of impact, a Christian woman needs to take her challenges, ideas, thoughts, fears, convictions, projects, and all her issues to God in prayer. Being in leadership for over three decades, as a Christian woman, I have seen challenges that only God could have sorted out for me. I have seen projects that were due to fail, turn around supernaturally, all because we prayed. I have seen God show up in my *quarter to shame* and rescue me from shame and reproach. I know and have felt the power of prayers answered.

I understand the power of Psalm 25. I have seen God save me many times from shame, disappointment and reproach. He has answered me in critical situations that I know that PRAYER HAS TO BE THE GREATEST SUCCESS SECRET THAT I HAVE.

Psalm 25:
'LORD, I put my life in your hands.[b]
[2] I trust in you, my God,
and I will not be disappointed.
My enemies will not laugh at me.
[3] No one who trusts in you will be disappointed.
But disappointment will come to those who try to deceive others.
They will get nothing.'

Prayer and worship have given me strength many times when I have been physically and mentally fatigued. So tired in fact that it was almost impossible to take another step towards my God given goals. But I got back up again and was stronger than ever.

Our Lord Jesus Christ in the midst of His busy schedule, would find time to step aside and prayerfully commit His day to God for direction and instruction.

I cannot emphasise how important it is for a leading lady to dedicate quality time each day for prayer, devotion, worship, thanksgiving and bible study. If you asked me to list seven most important things that a leading lady must do daily, they would be

1. Pray
2. Pray
3. Pray
4. Pray
5. Pray
6. Pray
7. Pray

Prayer is our life and prayer is our breath. A leading lady cannot lead, mentor, parent or progress without a consistent prayer life. There are no two ways about it. That is one part of our lives that we cannot negotiate.

A leading lady would not draft her year planner without prayer, she would not put a programme together without prayer. Many people close to me will have heard me say consistently that I AM AFRAID OF A PROGRAM, CONFERENCE OR PROJECT that I have not prayed about.

Venturing out without prayers is like jumping out of the boat without a word from the Lord. The only reason Peter could WALK ON WATER was because he stood on the word COME, which was in response to the prayers of the Apostles in a sinking ship.

Prayer has enabled us to meet huge budgets, even as a small ministry or small outfit. I remember one occasion where my ministry accountant, after he completed our final accounts, actually echoed my words, "Where did all this money come from?"

Prayer has enabled us to touch lives across cities and nations that I never dreamed I would touch my feet upon.

This life of prayer (of consistent prayer life) has baptised me with boldness to go where I would naturally be scared to go. I have said a few times, that as an introvert and shy person, I have been mistakenly judged as a core extrovert, perhaps because most times I am vocal about some of my thoughts. Deep within me and to those who are very close to me, they know that I am naturally shy and very laid-back person but it has taken the power of the Holy Spirit to push me in taking strides to move in the power of the Holy Spirit, in demonstration of His supernatural gifts. In my power and in my strength, I would do nothing but wait for life to happen to me - que sera sera.

Prayers have helped me listen to God intimately and to walk in obedience to the Lord's calling for my life. Some years ago, I recollect a dream where I entered a tunnel and pulled out around ten ladies from the dark. When they came out, they said to me "Pastor Marjorie, you only pulled out a few of us from the tunnel but there are loads of us still inside there."

While I was still wondering about who those ladies were, they burst out into a Chorus, clapping their hands powerfully as they sang. It was so heavenly and they sang without any musical instruments. The words of the song went like this - "Honour Him, honour Him, you have to honour Him because he came to save the prostitutes".

When I heard the song, I knew who those ladies were and right after I woke up from my sleep, I was worried. "Another mandate? Another assignment?" I said to the Lord. "No, I have too much on my plate already. I cannot take on another assignment".

My laid back nature likes to stay in the comfort zone but God empowered a side of me that wants to take the bull by the horns. Cut a long story short, through prayer and listening to the voice of the sweet Holy Spirit for over a decade now, I have taken a team each year to the two red light districts of The Haque, ministering one to one to the men and women in those districts. That could not happen without the power of prayer.

In a later chapter I will share more about our experiences of ministering in those districts.

Prayer, they say, changes things but I say prayer changes people too.

Through Prayer we have seen provision and divine supply for most of the projects we run as a ministry and as a family. God has been our divine source each time our financial brook dried up.

I remember several years ago when we needed to get a property for our first Church, having become frustrated by the caretakers at the school and community halls we used weekly for our Church services. We had reached a time when we were being moved from place to place and the members of the church were also as frustrated as us.

It was then that Pastor Clem went on a fast and his main plea to God was, "Lord bless us with a Church building as my fiftieth birthday gift." This was around three months after he turned fifty and as he ended his fast, he heard God. It was around 5pm that day and the message was for him to call a specific Estate Agent who God said would have a property for our Church.

To cut a long story short, the estate agent did have a D1 property for us but there was a snag; we didn't have enough money for the deposit for a mortgage and for all the repairs the building required as we got it prepared for worship. But we had our own plan and so we immediately began to draw up a long list of people to approach who may donate towards the property purchase.

We had our own plan but God had His and so He spoke to my husband and I. "Tear up that list and go to your church for the money." Seriously? What Church is Papa God referring to? Doesn't he know our Church?

However, because God Almighty was involved, we tore up the list and approached the church as the King of kings has spoken. To the glory of God, on that Sunday, we raised the sum required from the church, to make up the deposit and pay for the repairs. What a mighty God we serve. What an answer to prayer. Prayer works and a woman of influence must understand once and for all, in her heart, that God moves through our prayers.

I could share endless answers to prayers but for space we will end it here.

Here I would encourage you to take time to study the life and ministry of men and women who walked with God and who were people of strong prayer.

Men and women who pray understand the following things:

1. We have a relentless enemy. His name is Satan, Devil, or The Evil One as the scriptures sometimes refer to him.
   We have been commanded to pray.
2. Prayer unlocks the resources we require to fulfil our destiny.
3. The weapons of our warfare are not physical weapons but spiritual weapons of prayer and these are mighty through God.
4. The effective prayer of the righteous man avails much.

There are reasons why you need to study their prayer lifestyle and, why, as leading lady's we must pray.

1. They were men and women of passion like us.
2. They recorded proof of answered prayers.
3. They had result oriented prayers.
4. Prayer skills can be learnt and taught.
5. They knew how to wait in the place of Prayer like the Apostles of old. Acts 1: 4 They never attempted anything major or minor without waiting on God to seek His heart and opinion. Because of unity, the fire fell. A leading lady must understand the importance of praying before major decisions. Sad that in the scripture above, rather than listen to God, the Apostles felt they needed to cast lots, thereby limiting the God factor.
6. 'They mostly understood the power of prayer in the name of the Lord Jesus Christ.' Acts 3: 6 Peter and John said to the lame man, 'In the name of the Lord Jesus rise up and walk.' Not in their own names but in the name of Jesus, our resurrected Saviour. There is much power in the name of Jesus Christ so use it.

PRAYER PARTNERS

Let us have a word about the leading lady and her prayer partners. If you are married, your husband is your first prayer partner. However, it is also good to prayerfully find other female partners, mostly long-term friends who you know are not talkative or gossips and those who understand confidentiality. Take the prayer partnership step by step, testing their loyalty slowly before you release any highly confidential matters. I am a firm proponent of ladies having serious prayer partners but please follow the rules of engagement.

PRAYER IN THE MARKET PLACE

Taking a close look at most people in the bible and people throughout time who have made significant impact with great influence, I can tell you that they were men and women who mainly FOUGHT through life.

Name it from Abraham and Sarah, who fought barrenness. Moses fought Pharoah, David fought the Philistines and Goliath and Saul. Apostle

Paul wrestled with beasts and gospel opponents. The list goes on and on. Leadership and warfare go hand in hand.

How can anyone be promoted without breaking through the opposition? The leading lady must understand that the fight is real, otherwise she will give up on her hustle, her struggle and her assignment. Oh yes, I smile mischievously right now, ohhh, yes, the hustle is real. Very real.

Warfare is not a premise only for men as history shows us many examples of women heroines who have engaged in warfare. Although some of these are physical and extrinsic wars, today we must also face battles that are internal and could almost cripple a leading lady in her assignment.

The leading lady must understand that in her journey, she is not wrestling flesh and blood but wrestling against powers and unseen forces. These powers will mostly manifest as sorcery, voodoo, witchcraft, divinations and enchantments sometimes but the things you fight as a leading lady are not always visible. Sometimes, as leading ladies, we have warfare of the mind and so, we must know our enemies, which is why you should always pray through the list below because you can only win against an enemy that you have identified.

We are going to look at some of the internal and external wars that we face regularly, as leading ladies.

KNOW YOUR ENEMY

'Casting down imaginations, and every high thing that exalteth itself against the knowledge of God, and bringing into captivity every thought to the obedience of Christ;'
2 Corinthians 10:5 KJV

Lack of Self Esteem and Confidence.

This is a demon that most women deal with in life. It is an internal battle and personally, when this demon manifests against me, one of the things I do is silence it with the word of the Lord.

These voices tell us that we are incompetent, incapable and unworthy etc. That is because most women have learned this from our parents voices, insensitive spouses and authority figures who have told us lies about ourselves and when those voices from the past are not silenced they can take root and bring a leading woman down.

Shame

Shame was the first manifestation of the fallen man and it is one of the demons that leading ladies regularly fight against . What is shame? The dictionary describes it as the feeling of humiliation or distress, caused by the **consciousness** of wrong or foolish behaviour. Let me make a quick announcement here that may shock you. Everyone has been there and everyone has done that. If not for the blood of Jesus Christ, every one of us would stand up and raise our hands as guilty. You are not the first and neither will you be the last to have done wrong so dust yourself and fix your crown again.

Am I endorsing shameful behaviour? Not at all. However, if you have to lead with grace and bounce forward, you have to speak to both your consciousness and sub-conscious mind and remind yourself to forget the shame of your past. Christ died and sent it already into the sea of forgetfulness. Shame was the first manifestation of the fall in the garden of Eden.

As soon as man fell due to sin, the scriptures tell us that Adam and Eve realised they were naked and became ashamed. So, shame is an enemy that the leading lady must watch carefully. Otherwise, it can be a trap for slowing down. It can be a trap for enemy invasion and a ploy to take you back to where God has redeemed you from.

Competition

Many leading ladies have been trapped in the hands of this enemy, the subtle enemy of unhealthy competition with other women. As much as we would wish it, all fingers are not equal. However, all leading ladies are favoured equally but differently by the Lord. Just accept it as FACT that all fingers will never be equal. The parable of talent shows us how God blessed each one with different skills but according to our various abilities, no one got any less and no one got any more. Everyone got their talent according to their ability.

So, where then is the place for competition? I have often said that those who are competing with others really don't know the scriptures.

'I will make you exceedingly fruitful, and I will make you into nations, and kings shall come from you.'

Genesis 17: 6 English Standard Version

In the Abrahamic and Sarahic covenants, God included Kings as descendants. I wish that the brothers of Joseph had read that promise because if they had, they would not have sold Joseph to slavery. They would have known that each of them carried the anointing of Kings and Greatness. People who are in competition with others, really do not read the bible.

Another verse that we can quickly peruse is this:

'*There is* one glory of the sun, and another glory of the moon, and another glory of the stars: for *one* star differeth from *another* star in glory.' 1 Corinthians 15: 41 KJV

We can see clearly that every star has its own peculiar kind of glory as does the sun and the moon. We each have a glory of our own, therefore, your competition should be your past achievements as you strive to be a better **YOU**, each new season of your life and destiny.

Bitterness is evil

It's often said that bitterness can be compared to poison. It's like drinking poison but expecting it to kill someone else. This bitterness kills graciousness and no one can lead with grace, if they are bitter about life, people and events.

Ruth was a gracious leading lady. She dusted off her pain, bitterness and anger and chose to live a graceful life. It was her that gave Naomi the breath of life, after Naomi complained so bitterly about what life had thrown at her. Ruth made marinades from her life lemons and refused to be bitter.

Envy

Envy is a serious warfare that a leading lady must overcome. Envy is not Jealousy. God is said to be jealous for us but never in the scriptures is it said that God is envious. Jealousy in my understanding is looking out for what is yours, while Envy is wanting and lusting for what does not belong to you. In envy, you long for what someone else owns or has achieved and this makes you practically hate them for it.

We must always watch out for areas where we hate others for what they are achieving. Rather than hate, I would admonish you and remind you to learn from them and their principles of success, rather than being envious.

Envy is a cancer that is eating up the Church. This is an area where many leading ladies fail. Envy responds to other people's success by criticism, back biting, despising and bad mouthing. Once you see such traits in your life, as a Christian you must immediately stop and u- turn because envy and all the above heart sins, are such that they can hinder the flow of your success and clog your open doors and drain your anointing.

The fight for truth

I always want to look at truth from the viewpoint of Universality. Truth and principles to a leading lady in Christ, should be universal. What do I mean by that? A leading lady cannot hold a matter as truth and correct principle in one culture and setting yet hold it as false or untrue in another culture or location. Our truth and principles must hold true everywhere as leading ladies. This is a battle you must win even before it starts and if this is settled within your heart, then every time you are confronted with telling the truth, you will definitely not struggle because whatever holds true for you in private would also hold true in the open. This is how we create women of integrity.

Whatever you own that is true in one location and different in another location, is not your truth because it lacks integrity.

FEAR MUST BE CONQUERED

Every season of my life has presented fears that I have needed to conquer, almost on a daily basis. Every leading lady has her fears but she just must not own them. The list is endless, the fear of the unknown for finances, projects, family, health, welfare as we age. Fear of the children living their lives without faith in God through Jesus Christ. Fear of becoming irrelevant or the fear of losing money from investments. It is a long list and I am sure there are many things you could add to this list.

The issue of fear is a warfare that we must deal with daily from the living word of God to find our strength from bible verses that relate to each area of fear that is rising against us. That is why the fear references in the bible equal more than three hundred and sixty-five times and we can take at least one dose a day.

FEAR NOT sister. Make up your mind to fear not. Jesus is already in the future and he is in full control.

SPIRITUAL WARFARE

Have you ever heard the term, 'New Levels, New Devils?' As you rise in leadership, the battles become more intense. I once interviewed a young lady who was a successful entrepreneur here in England. I asked her casually if she had any success tips to share and these were her words. *"I entered the million pound profit zone so effortlessly in the years when my prayer life and time with God was strong and when I slowed down in my prayers, my profits dropped."*

This is what most Christian leading ladies do not understand or perhaps choose not to understand. There is spiritual warfare in the marketplace and most people you come in contact with daily believe and worship something. So, how dare you go empty into the marketplace?

When I was promoted to General Manager of Intercontinental Securities, many years ago in Nigeria, this was a reality that I took on board. I knew it was a competitive terrain. I knew it was God's hands that raised me up. I knew that I wasn't as rugged as most people in the industry and I knew I was the new kid on the block, so I had to seek power from the Holy Spirit.

I recollect calling my team at work and saying to them, "I know a secret to success. Prayer". I invited them to the church that I used to attend as a Sunday School Teacher in Children's Church. It was a Thursday night when we first met to pray from the hours of ten at night till five in the morning. Thank God they didn't think I had gone mad. Prayer and Bank executives? Yes, absolutely. Prayer and Bank Executives, why not!

We all got home after five in the morning, dressed and went to work as normal. That started our weekly seven hour prayers behind our other colleagues. Did we see supernatural results in our profits? Yes, unimaginable results actually.

Why did I share the story? Well, I am one believer in the fact that the spirit realm controls the physical. Just imagine our profits skyrocketing. We would call the clients from the North, South, East and West of the globe and we then entered into unimaginable profits for a company that was literarily run down.

So, a leading lady must always bear in mind that spiritual warfare is real and required for true success.

For four nights a week, I pray with a group of ladies into midnight and most of them are professional and highly skilled prophetic women in the marketplace. During these sessions, we pray into the midnight hours for two to three hours or more and yes, there were nights when these women did not want to leave the zoom space where we were praying.

Why do they not want to leave the prayer meetings? It is because we are seeing remarkable results in healing and transformations that result in strategic placements of these women as solution bringers in their spheres of influence. We are seeing our Churches lit up with God's fire and seeing the gifts of the Holy Spirit manifest through us in greater dimensions.

I would like to remind us that a leading lady must understand our fight is not natural. We do not wrestle against flesh and blood. There are powers that operate in the corridors of power and if you walk through these corridors, you must arm yourself with the right balance of prayer and bible study. You cannot be too busy to read the word of God and pray. Spirituality opens the doors to survival and thriving for a leading lady.

'For we are not fighting against human beings but against the wicked spiritual forces in the heavenly world, the rulers, authorities, and cosmic powers of this dark age.'
Ephesians 6:12 GNB

As leading ladies, we gain speed differently from other women in the world. I learned quite early in my journey of leadership that every career has a fast-track and I do not mean a get rich quick scheme. Nor do I mean a journey without a process. What I mean is a fast-track that is oiled by God and the Holy Spirit. The struggle, the pain and the hustle we go through is placed in a class that's almost enjoyable because at the end of the tunnel you can see the resurrection, the many corns and the victory that emanates from your death.

Just know this. Godly **leading ladies gain speed on our knees. Prayer is our fast track.**

Let's do a quick review of the verses below. Simply put, a leading lady gets to a point where she no longer operates from the soulish realm but moves to the realm of the spirit, where she gains heights and speed from the quickening Holy Spirit.

KJV 1 Corinthians 15:45 KJV
'And so it is written, the first man Adam was made a living soul; the last Adam was made a **quickening** spirit.'

'Like Elijah, we get to Jezreel before the "women" on horses.
(1 Kings 18:46)

Like the living creatures of Ezekiel 1: 14 we ride at the speed of lightening.'

This is the reason why our warfare must be on our knees. There's no other
way. We fight differently.

CHAPTER TEN

· · · · · · · · · · · ❖ · · · · · · · · · · ·

LEADING WITH SPIRITUAL AND EMOTIONAL INTELLIGENCE

What are the emotions that a Christian leading lady may possibly feel? I have decided to add this topic because, many times, people tend to think that leaders dropped from heaven. Even we sometimes deceive ourselves that we have no negative emotions. When we acknowledge our weaknesses, we are more able to overcome them.

Just like any other woman, leading ladies will most likely deal with emotional swings and pendulums of anger, fear, depression, love, hate, pride, envy, panic, physical attractions to opposite sex, lust, pain, joy, gratitude, hope, faith, excitement, peace and gladness, etc. The list is vast.

Listed above are some negative and a few positive emotions that we may encounter as leading ladies.

Here I bring to our remembrance the verse by Apostle Paul, admonishing all never to take things for granted. A believer must be alert.

1 Corinthians 10: 12
'¹²Therefore let him who thinks he stands take heed lest he fall.'

All these emotions both positive and negative, must be submitted to the Holy Spirit on a daily basis, so that we do not get entangled by them. Most often, the devil will wait for us to get on our high throne and then strike in the area of our emotions and spirituality. This is why we must scan ourselves daily and balance our emotions, based on God's word. When you notice any wrong emotions, never wait until they are full blown. Deal with them immediately. When Abraham took Lot, he was just a child, but Lot grew up. Woman of God things grow, so we deal with them before they do.

EMOTIONAL INTELLIGENCE AND THE LEADING LADY

When I began to pay attention to the subject of Emotional Intelligence, one of the things I said was how I wished I'd known some of these things earlier in life. The topic of emotional intelligence should actually be included in every Christian Leadership Course with a refresher required at some level each year.

Emotional Intelligence is the ability to have an understanding of your own emotions first of all and then the emotions of others. This is to enable you effectively serve people and handle problems in a way which puts you in the class of the matured leader. Through emotional intelligence and understanding of our own emotions, we can enhance our life-balance and the management of our life's assignment along with the life assignment of others who we lead.

Emotions are powerful and we cannot underestimate the power of strong positive and negative emotions in the life of the leading lady.

How important is emotional intelligence to a leading lady?

We all now know that the most intelligent, is no longer the most successful. IQ is no longer enough and we need to do much more and go that extra mile to succeed.

It is important that a leading lady understands the world is now a global village where any character mistake we make, will most likely go beyond our current sphere of influence. This is where self-control becomes paramount in our speech, relationships, actions, temper, choices and decisions. I am not propagating that we should be perfect, as we all are steadily walking towards perfection. Sadly, bad news spreads fast.

THE DOUBLE BIND AND EMOTIONAL INTELLIGENCE

Here I want to address the issue of the double bind, where it is likely that a leading lady does not realise she is unique in herself and therefore needs not lead like any other woman or like a man. She shouldn't be forced into the corner where she is competent but disliked because she is astute and determined or where because she is a caring leader, she is often seen as too soft. This is a catch twenty-two situation in which life expects women to be a certain way and when they are not meeting that expectation, they are disliked. It is important that a leading lady remains her true authentic self, always and avoid the catch 22.

In our authentic selves, we are able to manage our emotions and also understand those we relate to. This is one of the keys to make our leadership purposeful, meaningful and transformational. Leading women have to lead from both the heart and the head too. This is how we maintain good official, secular and personal relationships through healthy emotional intelligence.

John Mayer and Peter Salovey in 1997, coined the term 'emotional intelligence' and defined it as: -

"The emotionally intelligent person is skilled in four areas: identifying emotions, using emotions, understanding emotions, and regulating emotions."

In his book, **Emotional Intelligence why it can matter more than IQ,** Daniel Goleman expands on the work of John Mayer and Peter Salovey by identifying five key elements of Emotional Intelligence. Now, leading lady, let us look at these five elements briefly for a better understanding of the subject.

Self-awareness – Understanding your own feelings and how this affects your relationships with others around you.

Self-regulation - How you can regulate your emotions better so that you can lead better in different situations and assist those you come across in your leadership journey

Motivation - Controlling your emotions in seasons of testing, hardship, trails and challenges; Proverbs 24: 10 '¹⁰ If thou faint in the day of adversity, thy strength is small' KJV

Empathy - This is the ability and skill to see through the eyes of another person's emotions

Social skills - This is when you utilise key social skills to manage and navigate your way around relationships and to have a free flow in them.

With the background of Daniel Coleman's explanation above let's further explore how we can manage our emotions.

SOME WAYS TO MANAGE YOUR EMOTIONS

TRIGGERS

Everyone has triggers that can easily tug at their emotions negatively. A leading lady must understand her triggers at all times - In meetings, in public, in private, when dealing with spouses, children, family, friends and business associates etc.

Note them, conquer them.

'let us strip off every weight that **slows us down, especially the** sin that **so** easily **trips us up. And let us run with endurance the race God has set before us.' Hebrews 12:1 NLT**

EVENTS

There are tragic events that have the potential to trip us up and reduce our emotional alertness. Those dates remind us of painful experiences, disappointments, the death of loved ones, retrenchment dates and divorce for instance. A leading lady must watch out for those dates and anniversaries, so as not to trip.

FEEDBACK AND CRITICISM

How do you deal with negative feedback? Dear leading lady, watch your back. When people know what hurts you, they will give feedback to hurt you more and that can cause you to trip and experience negative reactions.

SUCCESS OF OTHERS AND THE VORTEX OF COMPETITION

This one is a girl thing. All girls, especially the leading lady has, to watch out for this. It is called the crabology, where all the crabs keep pulling each other down. You must separate yourself from the competition arena. Be your own competition. Stay focused and always compete with your last achievement, never another person. Desist from comparing yourself to others and avoid walking with the evil eye. Remember that most people, who you try to compare to, never show you their downsides. Everyone shows their upsides and victories on social media, so now you know that it's no longer worth comparing yourselves to others. You never know what's going on with them, behind the scenes, so don't get yourself into that competition vortex.

"But they are measuring themselves by themselves, and comparing themselves among themselves, are not wise". 2 Corinthians 10:12

SPIRITUAL INTELLIGENCE

As much as IQ (Intelligence Quotient) and EQ (Emotional Quotient) are important, I would consider SQ (Spiritual Quotient) much more important for us as leading ladies. It is often said that charisma and intelligence can open doors for us but lack of emotional and spiritual intelligence can crash a career, business or ministry in just one day.

The topic of spiritual intelligence is trending and many people are curious about what happens, beyond emotional and Intelligent quotient. After success in all their life achievements and smashing through the glass ceiling, many successful people are asking, "What next"? Many get all the success in their life ambition but they feel a gap in their soul and an emptiness in their spirit, despite all that they have achieved.

Spirituality is how we connect with the desires of our innermost self, our true self. The one that is not materialistic or selfish. That is where we, as Christians, begin to live a life that is controlled by the spirit of God.

Spiritual intelligence therefore is a power that we acquire through our connection to Jesus Christ as leading ladies and that adds meaning to our actions, values, emotions and intelligence. What's the use being intelligent and emotionally balanced without adding the dimension of spirituality? It brings all we do into the dimension of God, of selflessness, of faith and of eternity.

'For what does a man profit, if he should gain the whole world and suffer the loss of his soul? or what shall a man give in exchange for his soul?' Matthew 16: 26 Darby Translation

Therefore, life for a leading lady should go beyond the surface. Spirituality means we are dependent on God, relying totally on Him in all we do, say or think. We will then be women who lead by God's Holy Spirit who directs us day by day and in this realm of leadership, issues of the heart like forgiveness, gentleness, contentment, longsuffering, love for humanity and peace, become paramount. They take pre-eminence in our leadership styles.

Leading by spiritual intelligence takes us back to my initial chapter, where we defined leadership first of all as a journey where the leader is becoming that God personality. The one who is daily uncovering and discovering their true self. As you uncover your true self, you become a better person and become comfortable with who you are. You won't be intimidated by anyone else's success and you will simply become your own competition. At this level, the leader leads from a place of rest, confidence, integrity and, is therefore able to lead and raise other leaders from a place of her authentic self.

A leader who leads through spiritual intelligence is grateful for the leadership position she has attained, knowing that it is only by God's grace that she has been given the privilege to lead. A leading lady, therefore, must grow in the things of the spirit and daily crucify the flesh

'For to be carnally minded is death; but to be spiritually minded is life and peace.' **Romans 8:6** King James Version

So, what does it mean to be spiritually minded?

The verse below expresses it better than anything I could ever say.

'Then I looked and, oh! A door open into Heaven. The trumpet-voice, the first voice in my vision, called out, "Ascend and enter. I'll show you what happens next."'

Revelations 4: 1 Msg version

The leading lady who is spiritually minded will always look up. She will not look down at her circumstances, inadequacies, failures, struggles, critiques, unanswered prayers, competition or the enemy of her soul, but she will continue to look up, as that is where her help comes from. That is where the open doors are.

Of course, you got it. When we look up that is when our help comes - our redemption. How can you see the open doors if you keep looking down? You need to hear the prophetic call to your destiny, so always look up.

When we are walking in spiritual intelligence, we see the doors that God opens for us. We see the helpers of destiny that God puts in our lives. When God opens a door, nobody can shut it. This statement seems so simple but when you have dealt with a difficult and long-standing situation, where you needed to push for open doors, then you will better appreciate the door that God has opened by His power. One statement I often make is this:

"I am a woman who God helped."

I cannot tell you how the skill of looking up to Heaven and to God has opened doors for me. God has helped me in unusual ways. He has made me qualified, even when the world felt I wasn't qualified. He made me accepted when the world said I shouldn't be accepted and that is the result of looking up to God in prayers.

We cannot gain spiritual intelligence without an intimate solid relationship with the Lord through prayers and disciplined study of the word of God. It is in His presence that we learn to say no to the good ideas that aren't God ideas. It is in His presence that we learn who to associate with, to collaborate with and who to flee from.

Spiritual intelligence is our secret weapon for success.

Let's go back to our earlier verse from Revelations 4: 1

'Ascend and enter. I'll show you what happens next.'

Spiritual Intelligence gives us the power to ascend and enter to see what happens next. I could shout forever here. Isn't this what most people run around for and pay huge sums of money for? They want to see what happens next and here the King of Glory gives us access to ascend, enter, see and hear what happens next. Dear leading lady, this is the most beautiful gift we need. This is the most needful intelligence that we require. Let's seek it, pursue it and soak in it. It is higher than IQ. Higher than EQ. Higher than Political Intelligence and higher than Cultural intelligence or any other intelligence for that matter. Halleluiah.

CHAPTER ELEVEN

• • • • • • • • • • • ❖ • • • • • • • • • • •

BECOMING A THOUGHT LEADER AND MORE

Who is a Thought Leader? They are specialists in their field of operation and it is important, that as leading ladies, we pick an area of expertise. When you think about Dr Cindy Trimm, you think about Prayer, Leadership and the believers Kingdom mandate. That is her expertise. She is a thought leader.When you think about Cindy Jacobs, you think Strategic intercession so, what will we think when your name is called?

Thought leaders create and originate ideas through their knowledge and many life experiences.

They challenge the ideas of their peers and superiors biblically and theologically because they are well-read, versed and vast in their field of study.

Thought Leaders are avid readers.

They are not easily displaced in any sector where they operate but they make their mark in that sector.

They are drivers within their sector. What are you driving? Prayer, healing, wisdom, finance, health, parenting, teens, marriage, administration, leadership, women, real estate, entrepreneurship, advocacy? and pastors' wives? Once you recognise the area of your purpose and calling, you will need to be amongst the drivers in that sector of operation. A thought leader must be driving something.

They write books on their expert subject. Their work is well respected because it's not shoddy but well thought out and well researched

As a thought leader, you get on platforms as a speaker, interviewee, panellist and even become a newspaper columnist on your expert subjects.

They do top level jobs excellently, every time they are given an opportunity and they never cut corners.

They stay ahead of the curve.

When you become a thought leader, you no longer sell your products yourself because people sell them for you. You are mentioned in high places because of the subject that you specialise in and because you have gained respect among peers and superiors.

As a result of all the above, financial gains come to you. Every leading lady should aim to become a thought leader.

Emerging and intending thought leaders must be leading ladies who understand the power of trends.

They understand the flow of emerging trends within their sector and they do not underestimate trends. Instead, they cash into trends even if they are slow jumping into that trend. I had a conversation with Pastor Clem recently about Instagram and YouTube and we were talking about how we thought we already had too much work dealing with Facebook and Twitter and didn't need to get any more profiles going. We didn't need any more work and so, in the covid 19 pandemic lockdown and the flooding of Churches online, we suddenly realised that although we had a strong followership on Facebook, we lagged behind terribly on other platforms.

Thought Leaders watch Macro Changes

Thought leaders know what to do with the impact of macro changes within their sector and in this Covid19 and post Covid season, they will watch all macro changes. How is your ministry dealing with this new trend? How are you as an emerging thought leader dealing with digital changes and the barrage of online training and courses? These are trends that we cannot ignore.

GET VISIBILITY

Thought leadership requires that you get visibility though we must understand, that as Christian leading ladies, we are not showcasing ourselves but rather we are cities set upon a hill. They are different things. One is driven by the flesh while the other is a drive to glorify Jesus and to fulfil destiny.

PASSIONATE ABOUT SELF DEVELOPMENT

Thought leaders are passionate about self-development and passionate, not only about their own personal development but the development of others. Esther and her time of twelve months in the harem was a time of personal development, a time of cleansing, a time of purification, and preparation. Self-development prepares us for divine assignment. It is a place for discipline and self-motivation. A place of drive and as Christian leading ladies, we are expected to be self-motivated. This is a biblical expectation for all Christians and thought leaders too.

CREATE LEARNING ENVIRONMENTS

By creating a learning environment they provide am enabling environment. Many people have asked me how I know so much and do the many things that I do and I have heard them say *"Pastor Marjorie is so intelligent"*. To some extent, I admit a bit of this to the glory of the Lord.

However, I have often said that my environment is a very enabling environment for learning. As I grow in leadership, I am a student of many thought leaders that have mentored me, to never ignore the importance of learning through every means possible. These thought leaders are aggressive learners and they aggressively pull others to learn.

What do people say when they hear your name? What subject are you known for? Name any great man or woman dead or alive and you will recognise one running thread through each of their destinies. They all have a subject of speciality and they are avid learners. So dear leading lady, what is your area of specialisation? If there is none, then this is the time to start building it. Learn it, develop it, study it, fan it, live it and BE IT!!!!

May the spirit of innovation rest upon you right now in Jesus mighty name

Proverbs 22:29 (New King James Version)
"Do you see a man *who* [a]excels in his work?
He will stand before kings;
He will not stand before [b]unknown *men*".

Exodus 31: 1-6
"Then the LORD spoke to Moses, saying: [2] "See, I have called by name Bezalel the son of Uri, the son of Hur, of the tribe of Judah. [3] And I have filled him with the Spirit of God, in wisdom, in understanding, in knowledge, and in all *manner of* workmanship, [4] to design artistic works, to work in gold, in silver, in bronze, [5] in cutting jewels for setting, in carving wood, and to work in all *manner of* workmanship.

[6] "And I, indeed I, have appointed with him Aholiab the son of Ahisamach, of the tribe of Dan; and I have put wisdom in the hearts of all the gifted artisans, that they may make all that I have commanded you"

HOW CAN YOU GROW AS A THOUGHT LEADER?

I would recommend some of the things I decided to do on my pathway to becoming a thought leader.

Create your personal Board of Directors

I have a good network of people that I work with on various issues. Some of them are friends that I have known for many years and some are people I have met in the course of my work and ministry but, within this group of people, I have intentionally chosen a core group whom I secretly refer to as my personal board of directors. Are they aware that I refer to them as such? No not really.

But these are people from different walks of life, with diverse experiences in work and ministry and I believe that they are in my life for a purpose. I would consult with them (after praying of course) before any major decision within my work.

"But in the multitude of counsellors there is safety." Proverbs 11: 14 KJV

I cannot tell how much these ladies have pulled into my life and ministry. There is always safety in the midst of counsellors. One bible version (Berean Study Bible) says it all, "but with many counsellors comes deliverance"

DON'T OVERLOOK YOUR TRANSFORMATIONAL CRUCIBLE MOMENTS

During my leadership course two years ago at the Said Business school of Oxford University (I must confess that is one of the most fulfilling things I have done in a long time, outside Church life), I was introduced to the concept of the transformational crucible moment.

What's a transformational crucible moment?

In my own words, these are moments in your leadership journey that you thought would crush you but instead, they strengthened you and caused you to be stronger. Everyone has those moments. It was interesting to reflect during the course about some of those very crucible moments that have helped to shape me to the woman I am today. I am not much of a sports or fitness person but if I was, I would have simply said that these are moments when my leadership muscles became firmer, stronger and more visionary.

One very important crucible moment for me, was my shift from being a merchant and investment banker to the Church sector and this put me in a situation where I had to serve as a minister's wife, alongside my husband. I came to the realisation that, although women have almost 70% of the volunteering roles within churches, they were not fully represented in core leadership roles across many denominations.

Although I had come into the new role with a lot of transferable skills from my banking days, I found that my leadership was usually questioned and subverted. People were comfortable with me doing jobs but not with a decision making role.

Then it dawned on me that there would be many other women in that situation who were silent and without a voice and had been suppressed within the church to do back side roles but without decision making roles.

As a result of this, my husband and I were inspired to start the WISE WOMEN AWARDS in 2004 and this award showcases the works of leading Christian women who are working within and outside the Church world across all denominations, to encourage women to push beyond the Church walls. Today, The Wise Women Awards runs annually in West Africa, the UK and Europe, with hundreds of women awarded in the past seventeen years.

One of our strategies is to invite prominent Christian men and women who, through their stories at the awards ceremony, can help to change perspectives. I am glad that this particular transformational crucible moment activated a lasting change within my community.

Having had several crucible moments as a Church Minister, they became situations that challenged my faith as a woman in leadership but each time, God turned it around to bring good out of the situation. You may now need to take a few minutes and reflect on a couple of your own transformational crucible moments to see how these have changed you and helped you become better.

Moving to England from Nigeria around twenty-six years ago was another of such moments for me. Coming from a healthy competitive background to a non-profit environment (Church) was truly challenging. Leading and working with paid motivated staff to leading volunteers was not one of the easiest things to do. There were moments when I escaped into my shell but a time came when I decided I needed to self-motivate through the power of the Holy Spirit and the grace of the Lord. Through self-motivation and self-encouragement, I have been able to mobilise active and very well motivated volunteers who now support the work I do at various levels.

Covid 19 was a transformational crucible moment for all of us. We learned the skills of technology. We took our events and church services online. We shopped more online which is, something I never liked. I practically zoomed myself out doing Zoom meetings, prayer meetings, workshops, seminars, coaching online and the peak for me was the sixteenth Wise Women Awards online on Zoom, Facebook and YouTube in the year 2021. The lessons from Covid19 are innumerable. They are countless. We slept and woke up completely different in our thinking patterns and our life values changed around friends, family much more than ever before.

UTILISE REVERSE MENTORING

Mentoring is one of the approaches that has helped me support my peers and those who are younger in age and experience to me in their leadership journey. I have mentored informally and sometimes formally, all in a bid to help others achieve their full potential in Christ. I have also been mentored at different levels of my life by many and of course, let's not forget my greatest mentor Jesus Christ, my Lord and Saviour, through His Holy Spirit. Where would I be without Him? Jesus and the Holy Spirit are and will always remain the greatest mentors ever. What a privilege we have as children of God

"But the Comforter, which is the Holy Ghost, whom the Father will send in my name, he shall teach you all things, and bring all things to your remembrance, whatsoever I have said unto you." John 14: 26 (KJV)

I am also glad to say that my mother and father were my first mentors. They taught me the art of self-confidence, praying lifestyle, contentment and integrity.

I consider myself a proud product of those two completely opposite humans but I am glad I could learn from both of them. I am also a product of Pastor Clem's strong biblical mentoring, prayers and love.

My spiritual parents have been of immense support with prayers and strong biblical mentoring. Having said all of the above, you can see that I am a strong advocate for mentoring.

A few years back, I was helping a young lady who had approached me for spiritual mentoring. We became quite close and would speak about life, money, leadership, faith and family, among many other things and then, at some point I realised that I was being mentored by her in some way. I got worried. Why? Well, my notion of mentoring was upwards to downwards and now, I was seeing the reverse in some aspects and I thought that was very unhealthy.

I prayed about it and God said - "Reverse Mentoring." I had never heard those words before and so I googled them and there it was, as a management principle. Whaooooo.

Mentoring should never be a one-way street. There is always much to learn from the younger leaders in our circles.

Daniel mentored the kings of Babylon and Medes and Persia, as he was used to interpret their dreams and direct affairs of their Kingdom. Joseph was used to mentor Pharoah on how to direct affairs in the Kingdom.

Today, there are things the younger people know that the older generation do not. As leading ladies, we must make a conscious effort to ensure that the younger generation are around us to learn from us, to be mentored by us and in the process, once in a sometimes use reverse mentoring to learn from them too. They understand their generation better and understand the tools and methods that can reach them better. Let's not be afraid to learn from younger leaders. Reverse mentoring should actually be an intentional leadership strategy and a Christian leadership strategy.

Imagine if Naaman's wife didn't listen to the maid and imagine if Pharoah didn't listen to Joseph. Imagine if Naaman didn't listen to his servant.

APPENDIX

FINAL NOTE

Now that you have read **THE LEADING LADY HER LIFE AND HER INFLUENCE** please do not put it away on a shelf and forget about it. Take the time to look at your notes and thoughts from reading this book and ensure that you are taking active, decisive and significant steps towards a life of greater influence and impact.

You can take further steps by making a decision to contact Pastor Marjorie O Esomowei and join her Mentoring, Training or Coaching Sessions- admin@wisdomforwomeninternational.org

APPENDIX

OTHER BOOKS BY PASTORS CLEM AND MARJORIE ESOMOWEI

To purchase these books and other products by Pastors Clem and Marjorie Esomowei Please visit
www.triumphant.org.uk or www.wisdomforwomeninternational.org

Children are like Olive Plants	Pastor Marjorie Esomowei
Overcoming in Gilgal	Pastor Marjorie Esomowei
33 Great Tips for Single Ladies	Pastor Marjorie Esomowei
A- Z of the Multipurpose Woman	Pastor Marjorie Esomowei
Designed for the Palace	Pastor Marjorie Esomowei
Inspirational Business Ideas	Pastor Marjorie Esomowei
No More Curse	Pastor Marjorie Esomowei
The Successful Christian Business Man and Woman	Pastor Clem Esomowei
Davinci Code …Truly Fiction	Pastor Clem Esomowei
Divine Decrees 1V	Pastor Clem Esomowei
Making Progress	Pastor Clem Esomowei
Victory Over Offences	Pastor Clem Esomowei

APPENDIX

ABOUT THE AUTHOR

Reverend Marjorie Esomowei is a certified Coach, Trainer, Mentor and Speaker. She is the author of several books and study manuals. She is also a graduate of Economics from one of Nigeria's premiere Universities, Ahmadu Bello University Zaria and an Alumni of the Oxford University Said School of Business. Before joining her husband in full time Church Ministry, she was a very successful Investment Banker.

Marjorie is an ordained minister and Co-Pastor/ Founder of Triumphant Church International in London, England. She and her husband of over thirty-five years, the Reverend Clem Esomowei, minister together, having Apostolic oversight of Churches and outreaches in the United Kingdom, Europe, South Africa and Nigeria. As a profound teacher of God's word and a prophetic intercessor, her ministry is characterised by signs and miracles.

She is the president and founder of the dynamic **WISDOM FOR WOMEN INTERNATIONAL, W4WI** the prolific **WISE WOMEN AWARDS, COMFORT HOMES CARE FOUNDATION and ILEAD ICHANGE AND IINFLUENCE, which is the mentoring and coaching arm of W4WI.**

A dynamic, proactive, ingenious and resourceful woman. Pastor Marjorie is a natural leader whose abilities have been enhanced with almost forty years of being in leadership, both in the Ministry and the marketplace putting her in the league of sought after International conference speakers.

Pastor Marj as she is very fondly called has since the early eighties served with distinction in numerous leadership capacities with a unique style of strong leadership blended with caring competence and a very large heart. She is known to be at ease with the very powerful and the most humble.

Recently listed on the Keep the Faith magazine hall of twenty Most Influential Black Christian Women in Great Britain, Pastor Marjorie is a recipient of several awards and has made appearances on BBC, ITV, and many Christian TV, Radio channels and print media.

A loyal friend, mother, pastor, coach, mentor and confidant to many, and continues to so readily and willingly give so much of herself through her ministry, prayers, service, giving and love.

Lightning Source UK Ltd.
Milton Keynes UK
UKHW010614070622
404054UK00001B/31